AF569772

I ONLY HAVE EYES FOR YOU

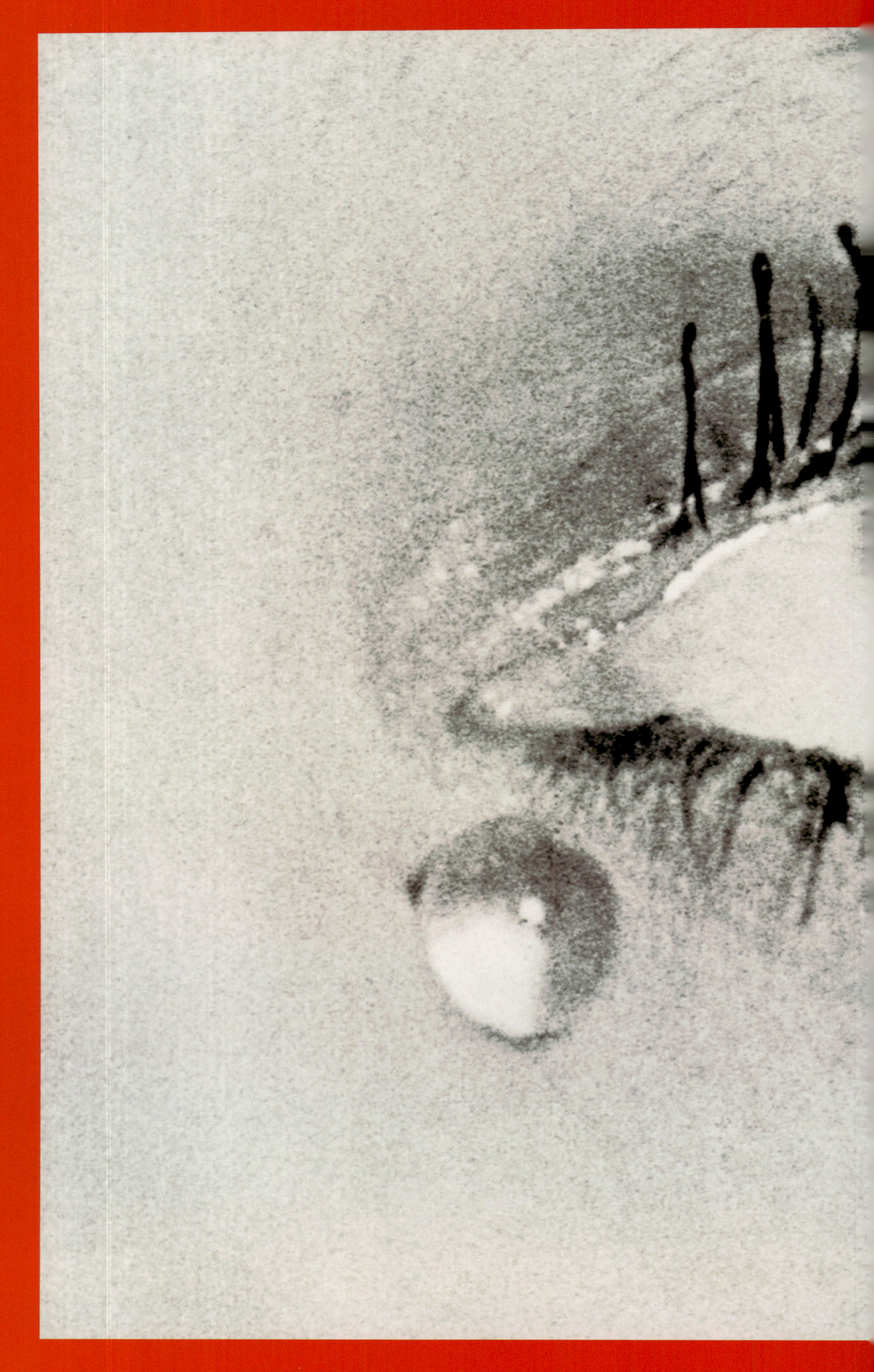

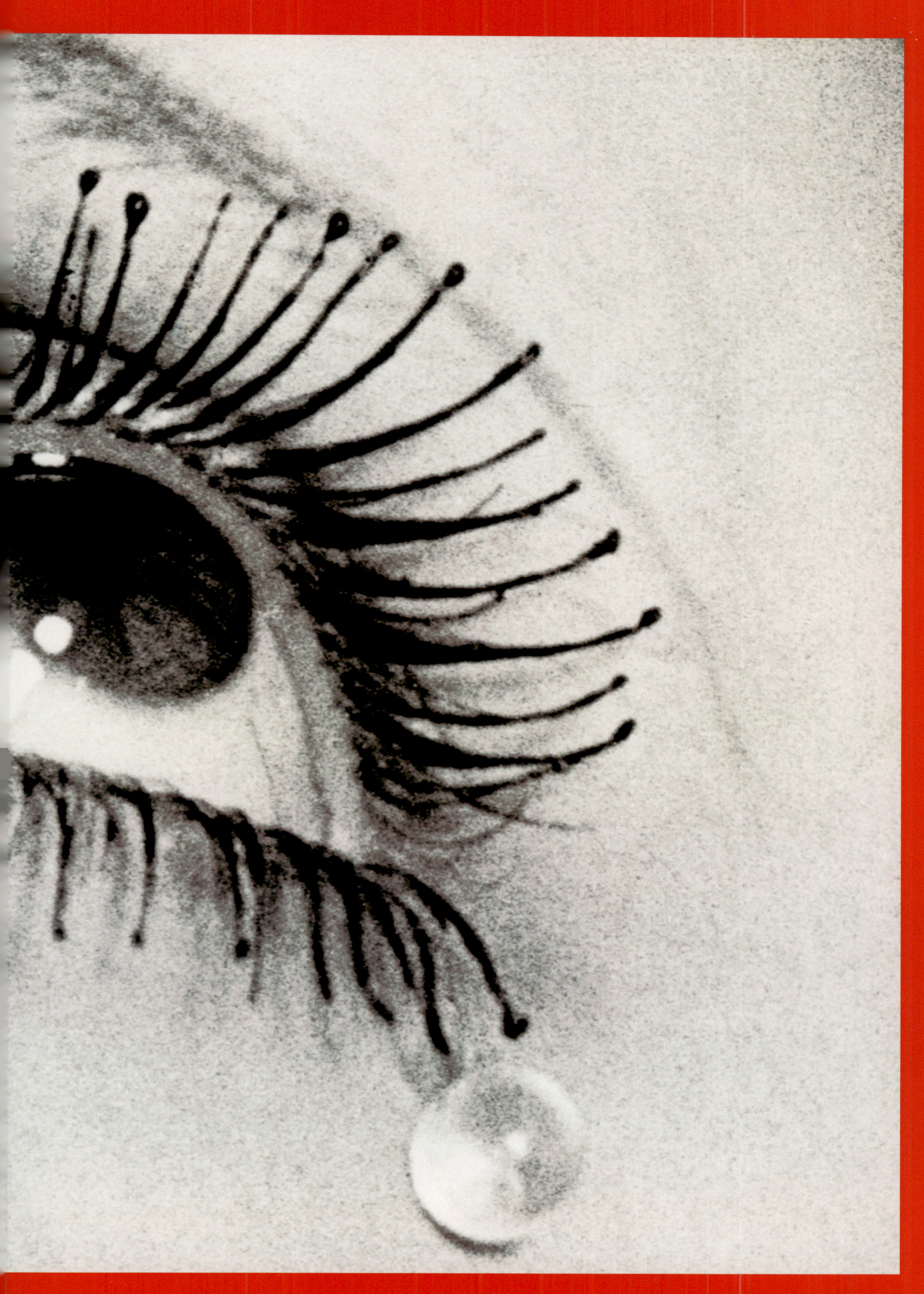

To my daughter, Samantha:
Your beauty, style, grace, and love
is the source of my endless happiness.

To my son-in-law, David:
I am so proud of the man and husband you are...
I am thrilled for our future together.

I love you both so very much!

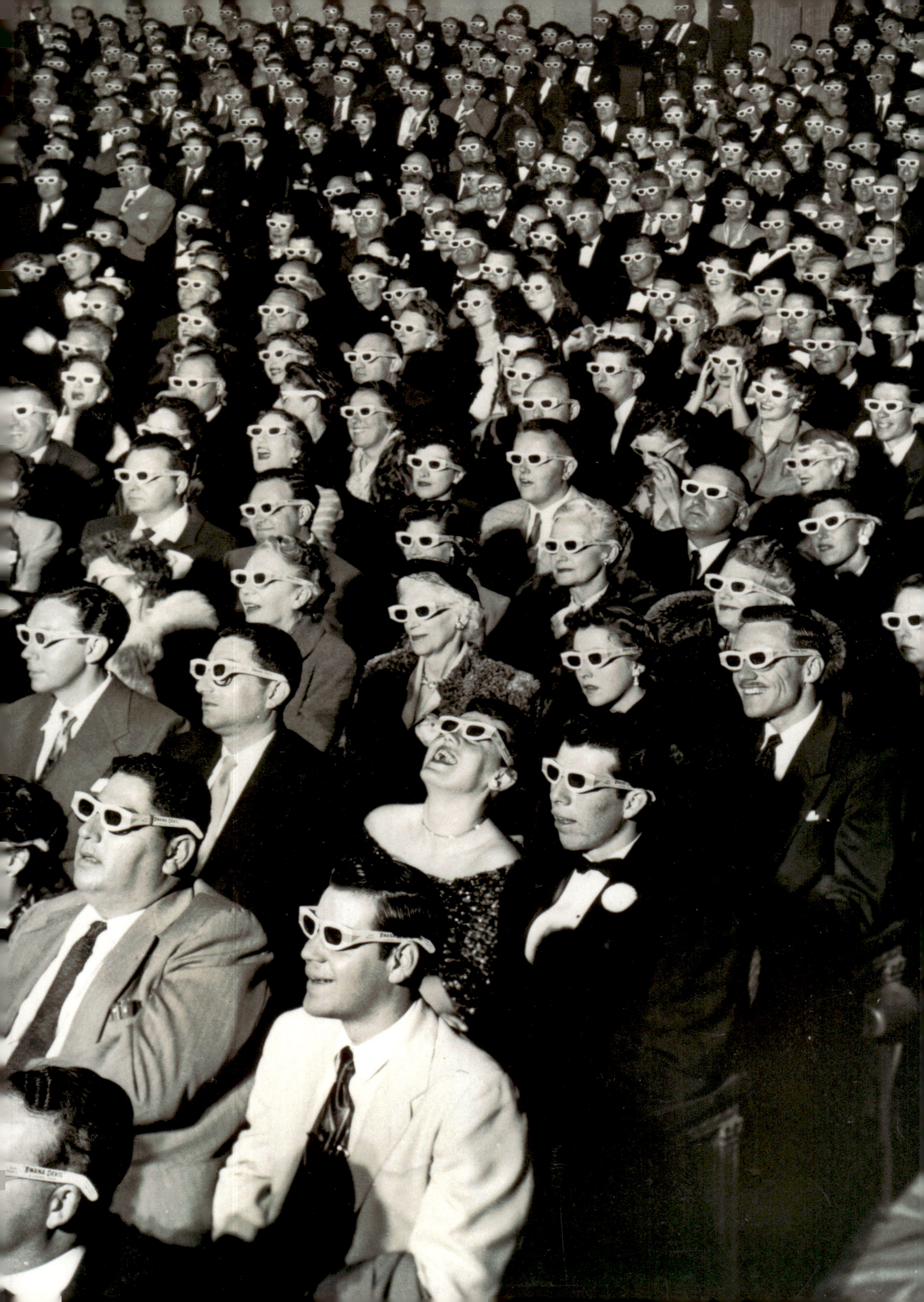
BWANA DEVIL

I ONLY HAVE EYES FOR YOU

Alice Harris

Introduction by Christian John Wikane

Photo editing by Sarina Finkelstein

pH powerHouse Books Brooklyn, NY

Eyes have their own language. At times, they're more powerful than words. From seductive stares to alluring glances, *I Only Have Eyes for You* illuminates the beauty, glamour, and mystery of eyes. Acclaimed author and style innovator Alice Harris has selected a breathtaking collection of iconic photographs and stunning artworks that capture all the magnetism, sensuality, and sophistication we see in a flash of lashes. In the pages of this chic and stylish tour through unforgettable images, the world's most celebrated visual artists portray eyes in all manner of repose, whether magnified by makeup, coyly peering through masks, or piercing the page with a penetrating gaze. *I Only Have Eyes for You* continues the brilliant and inspired artistry that Alice Harris authored in her most recent book *Blow Me a Kiss* (powerHouse books, 2014), as well as *The White T* (HarperCollins, 1996), *The Blue Jean* (powerHouse Books, 2002), and *The Wedding Album* (powerHouse Books, 2006).

— Christian John Wikane

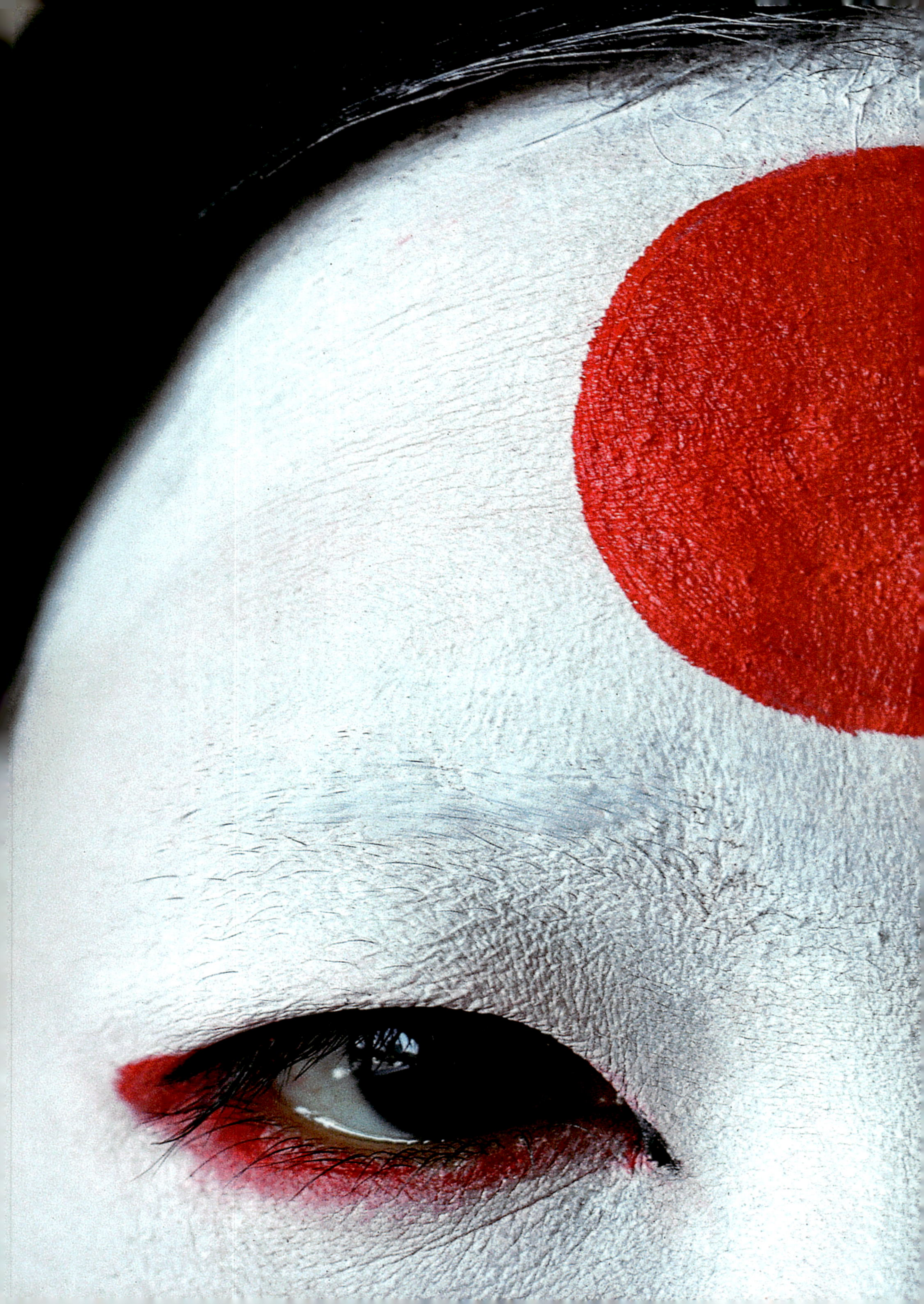

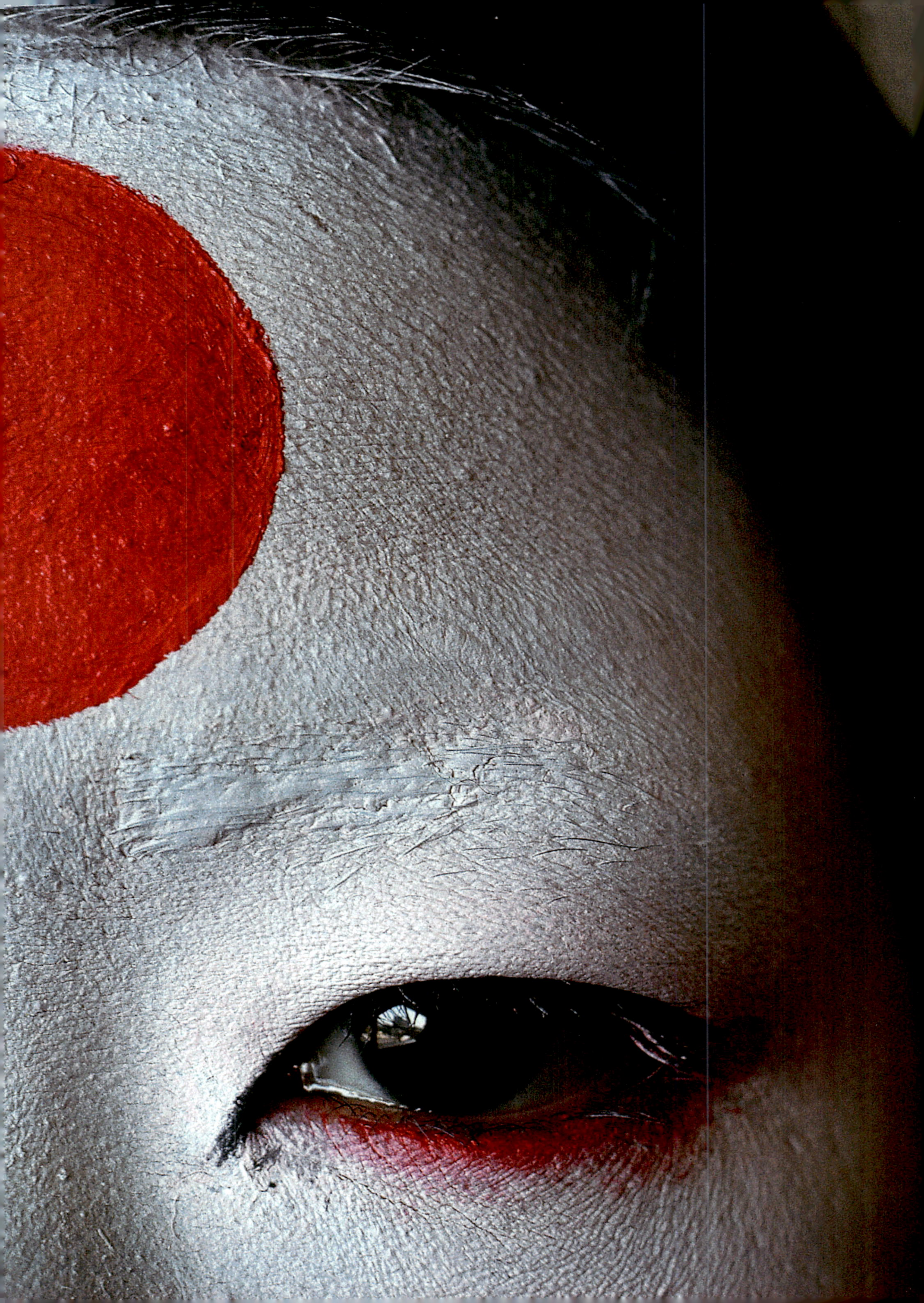

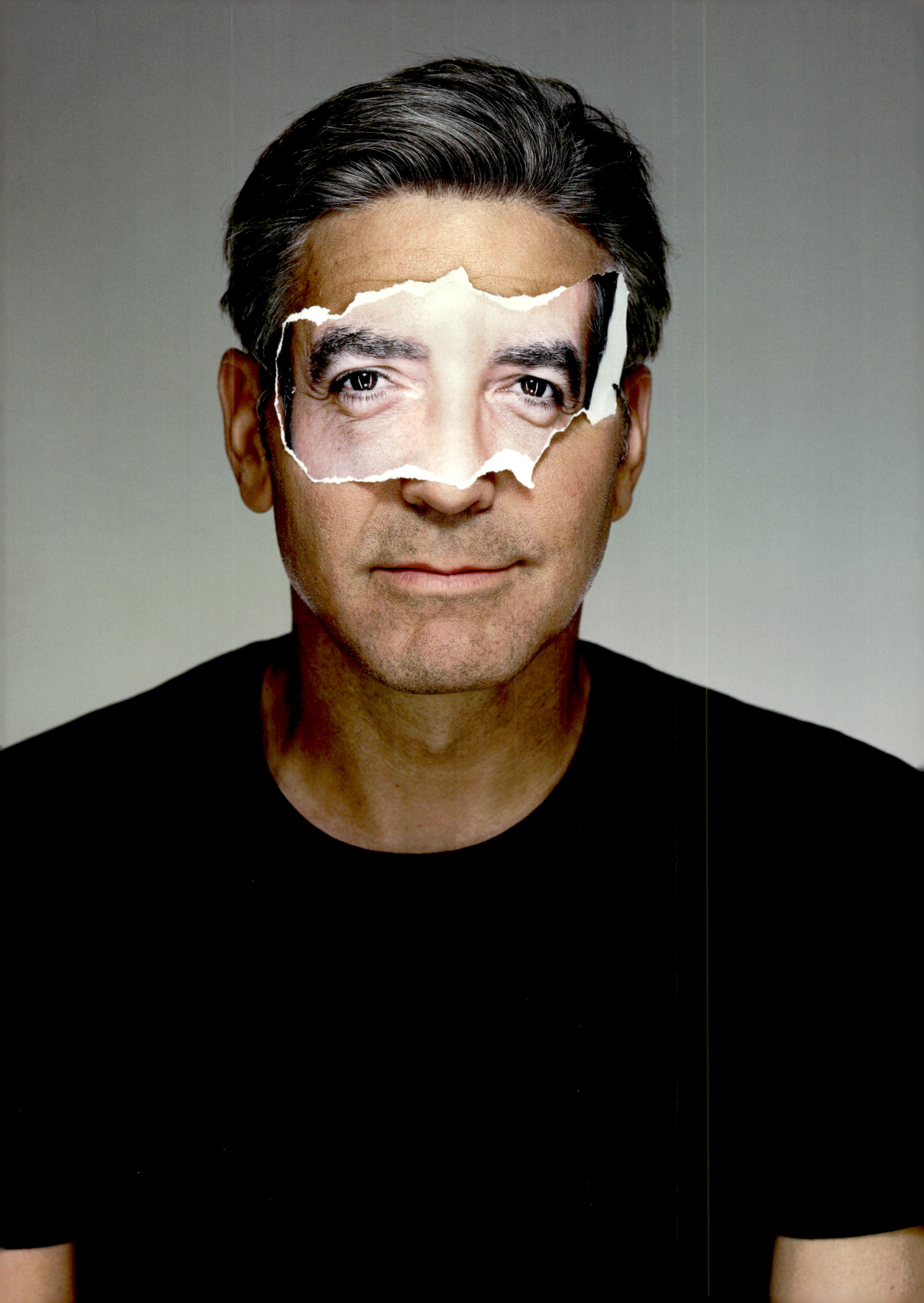

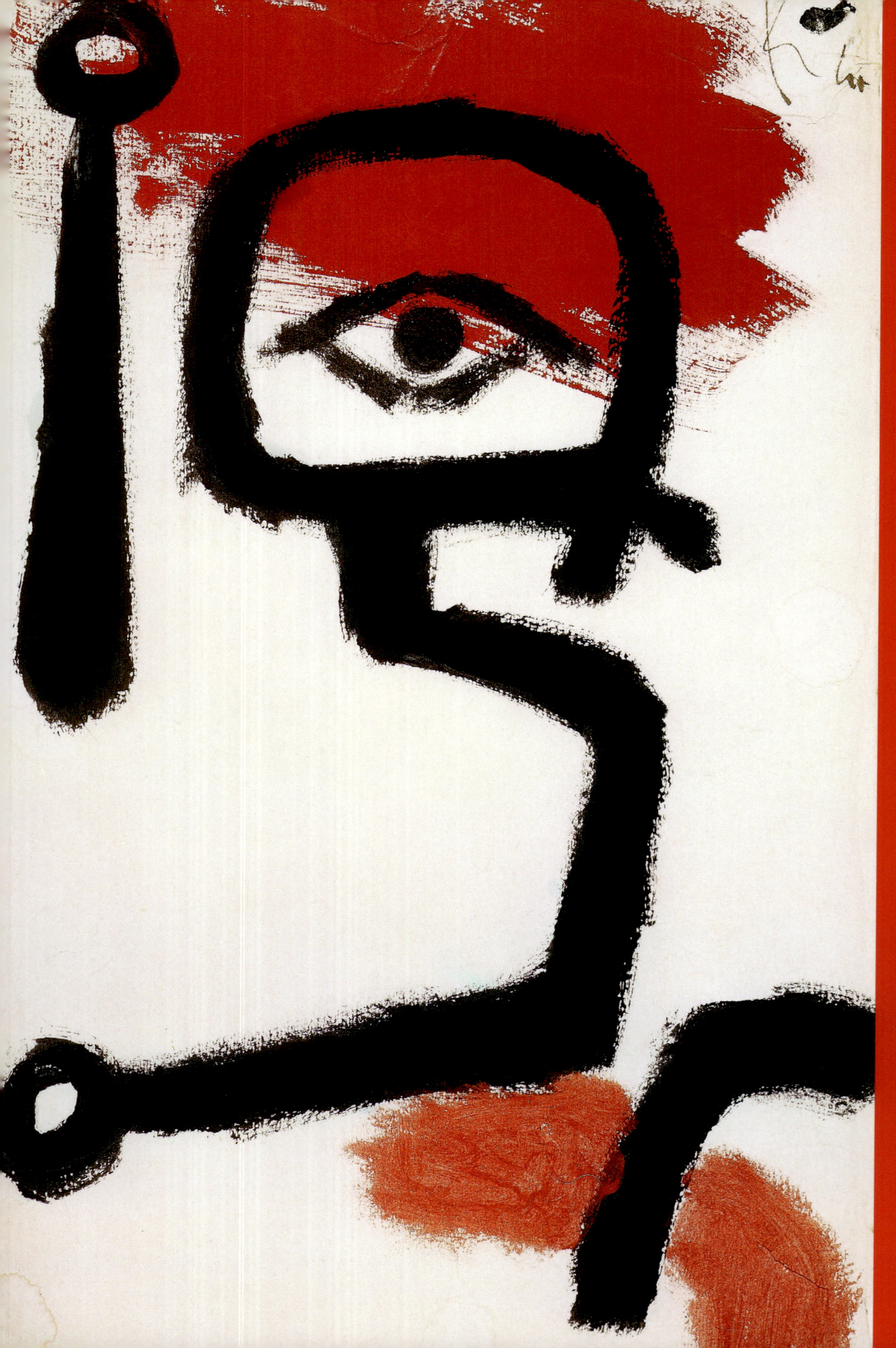

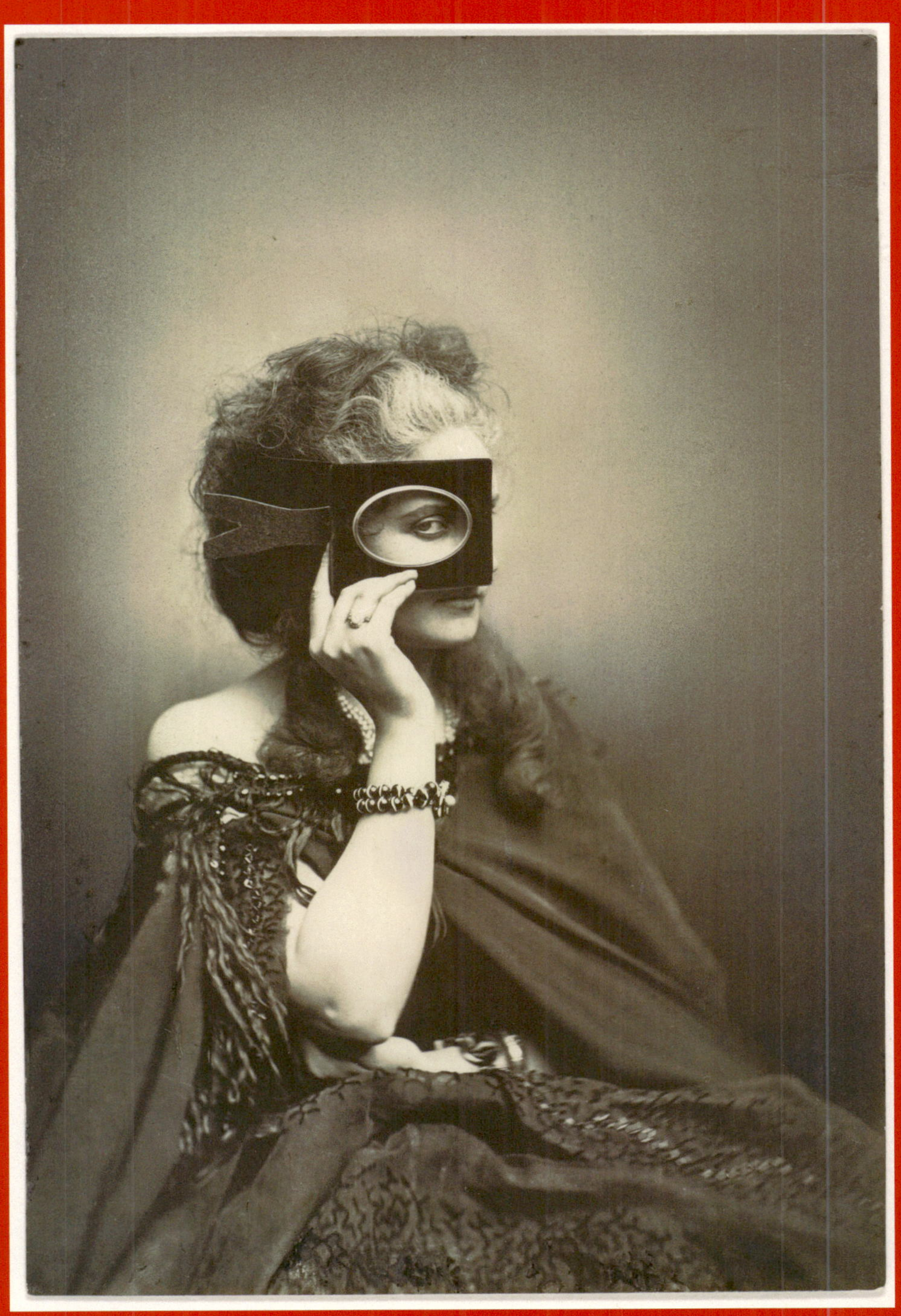

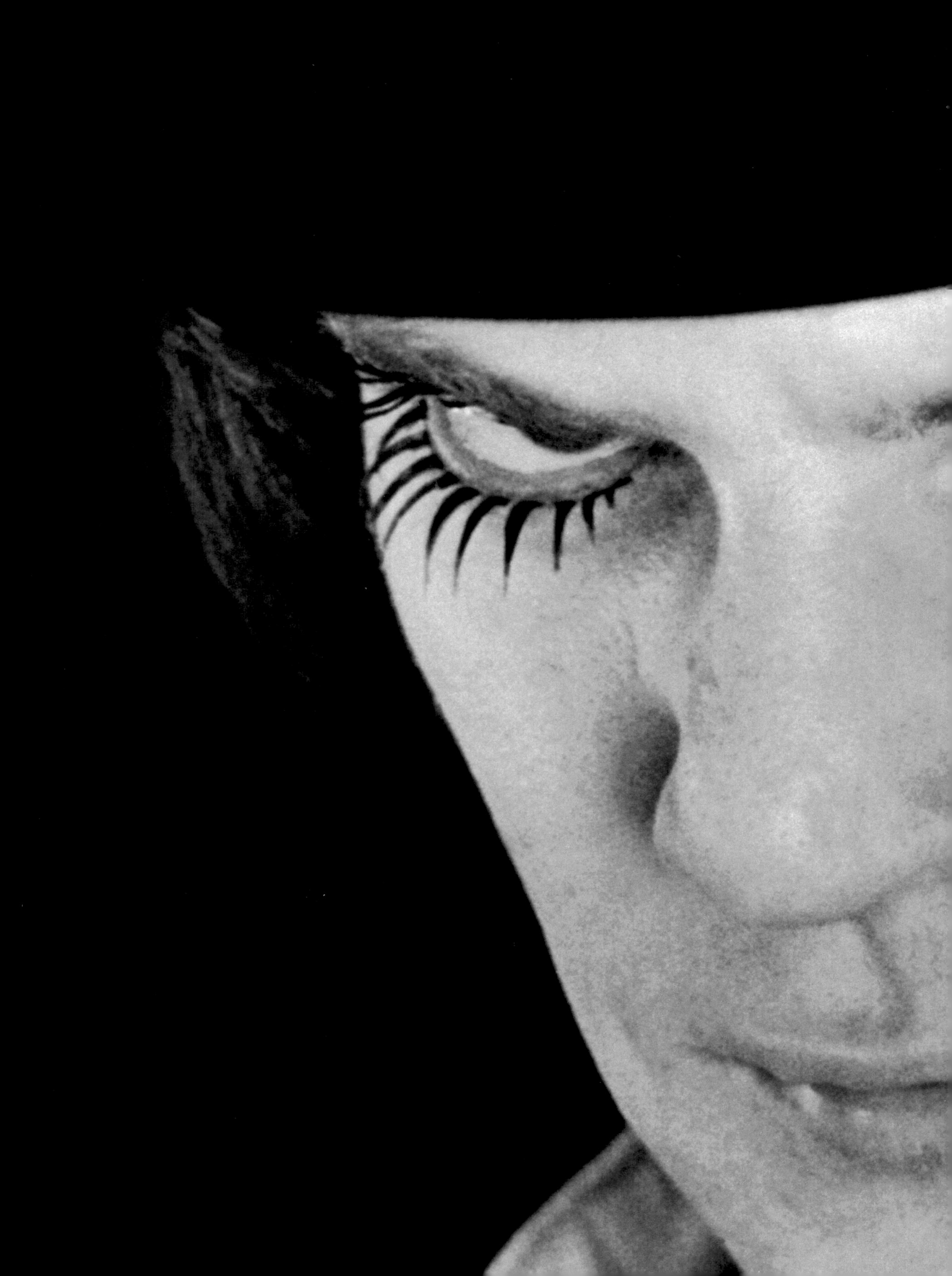

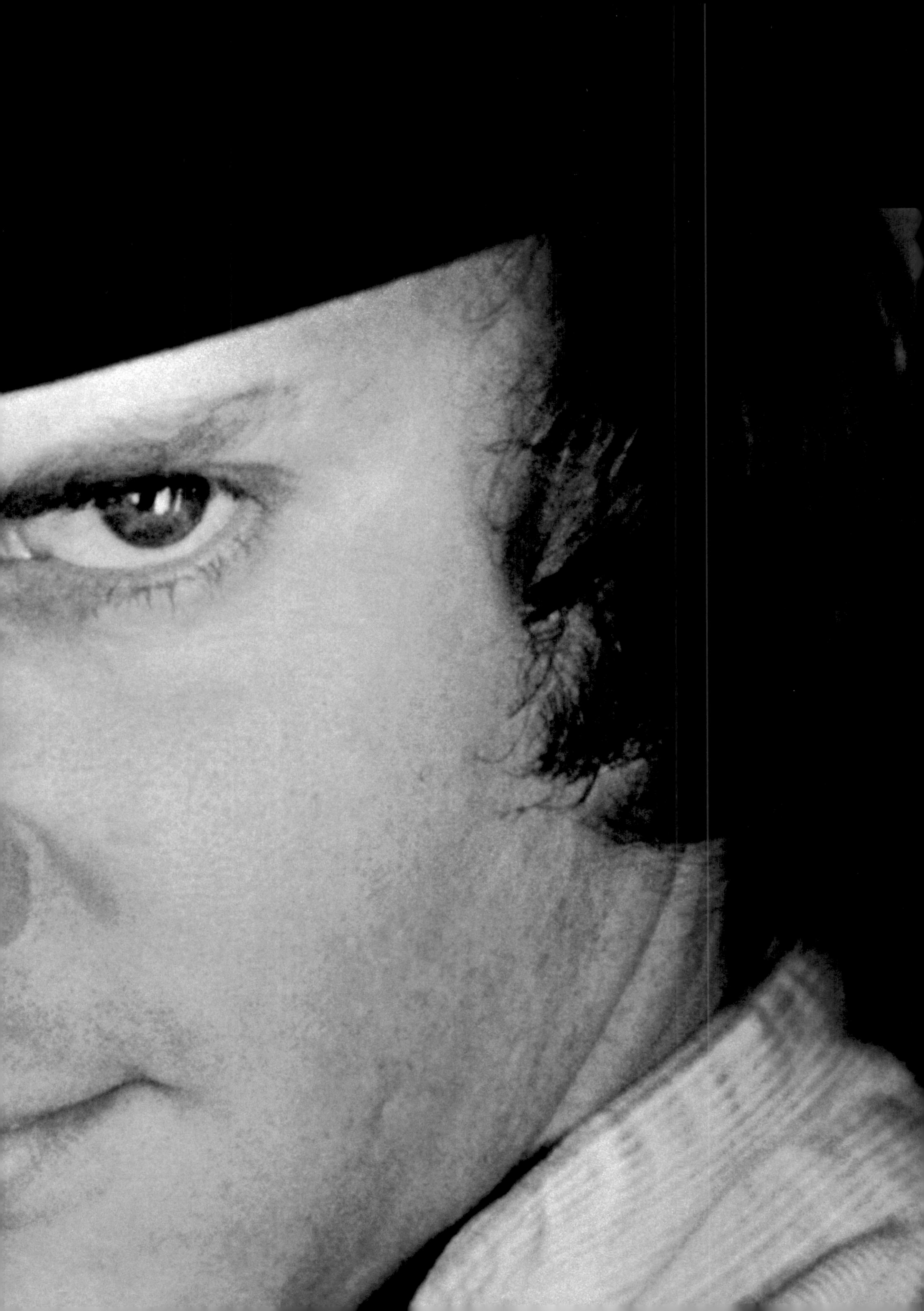

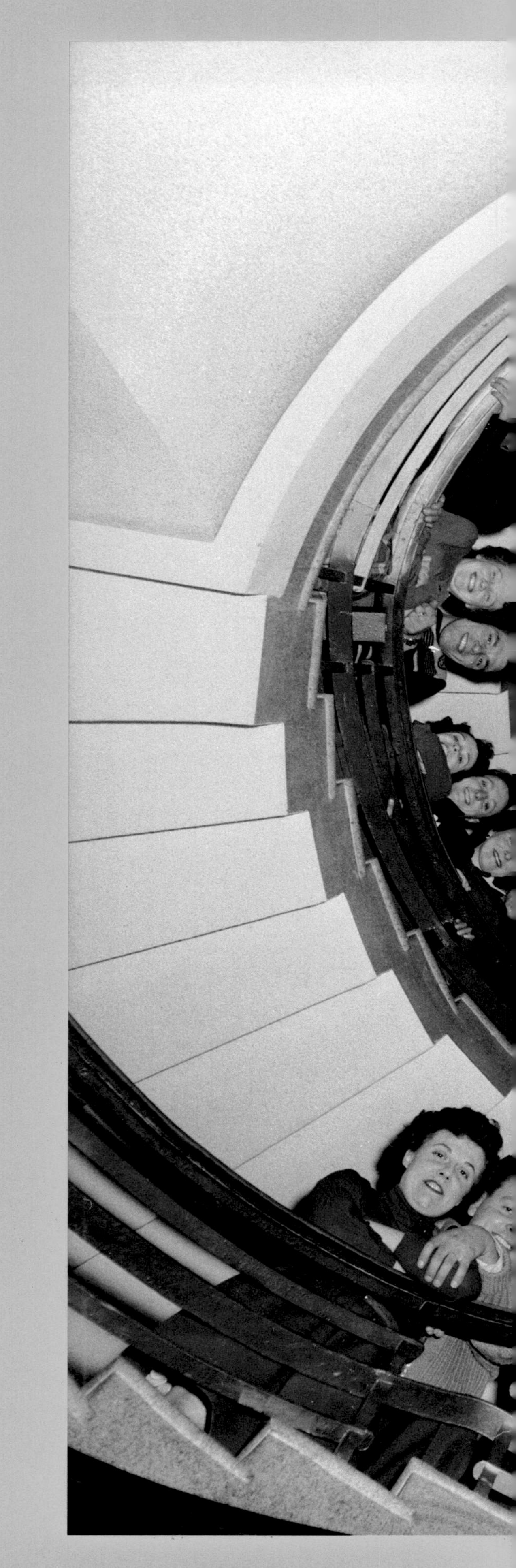

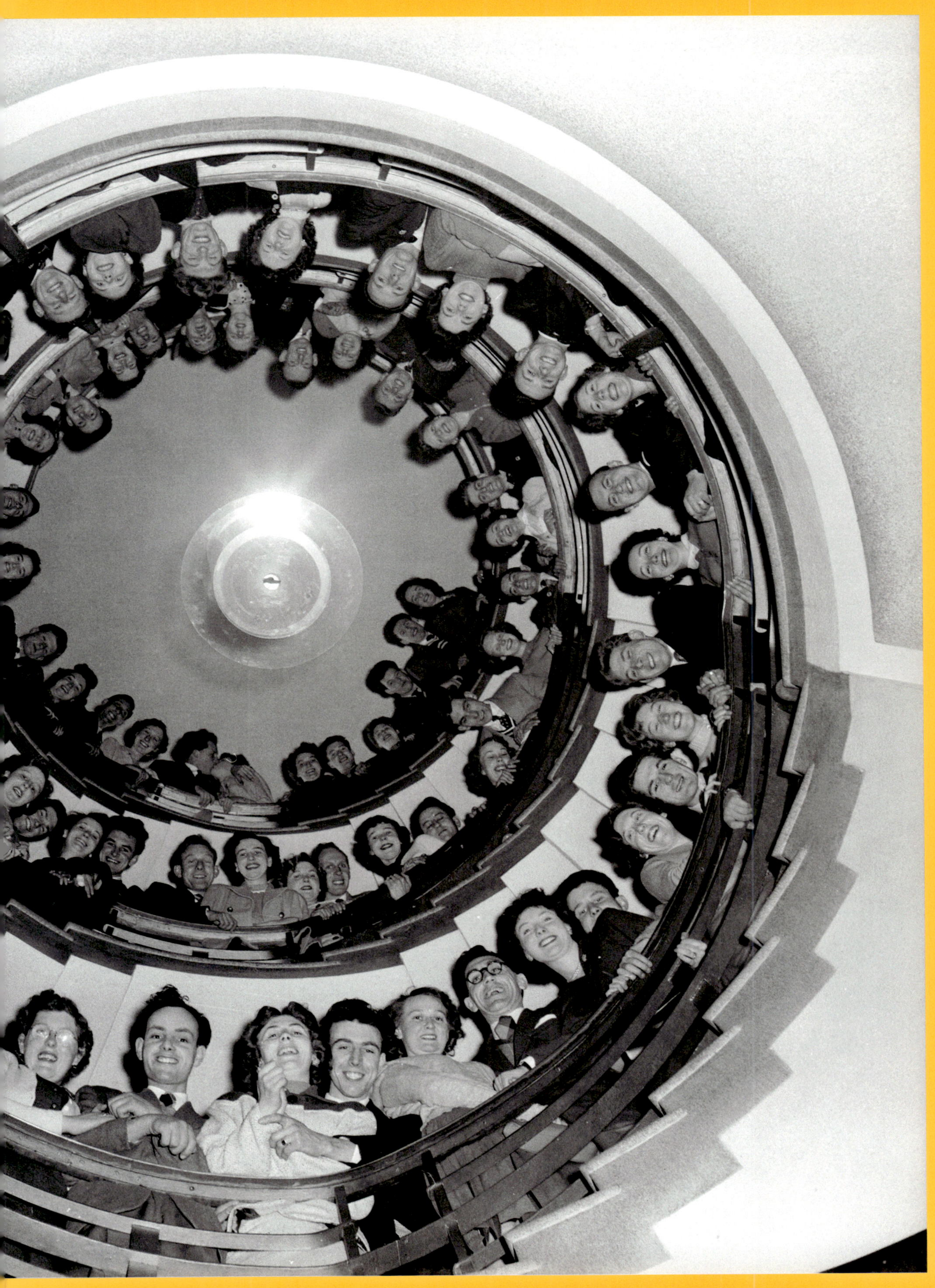

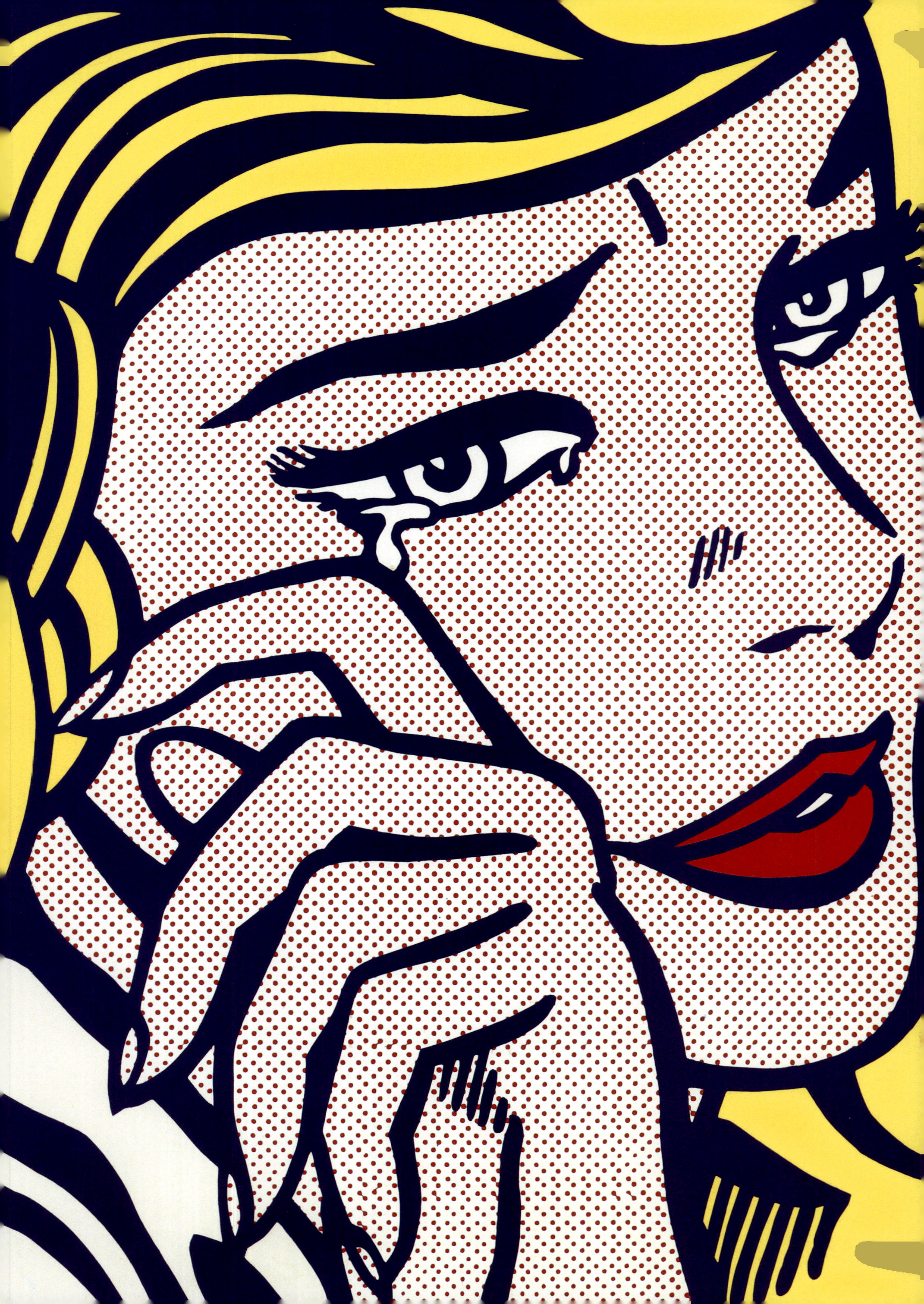

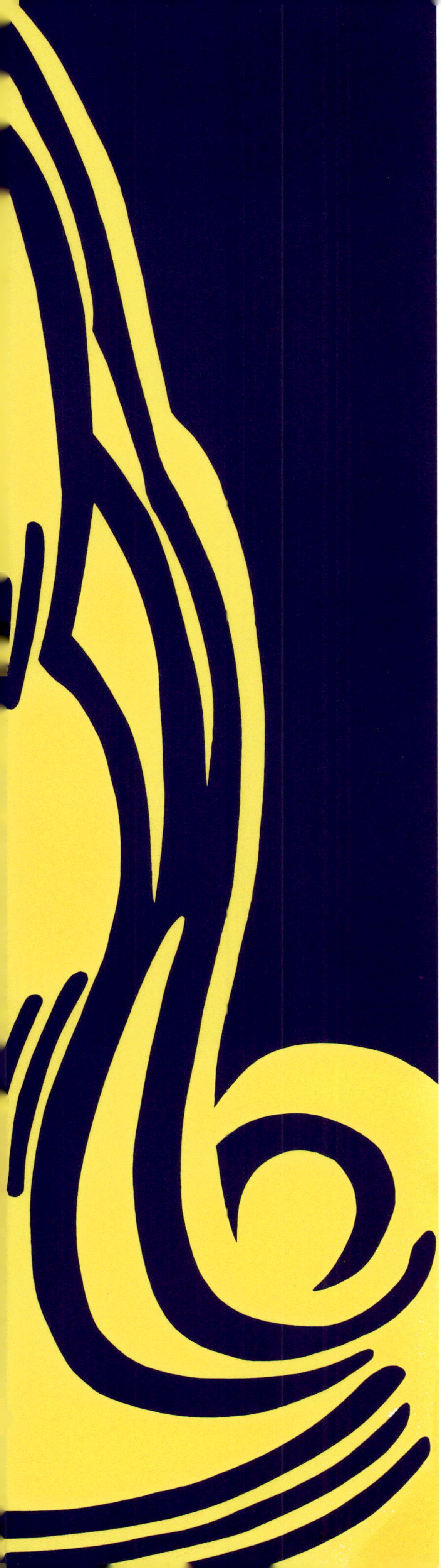

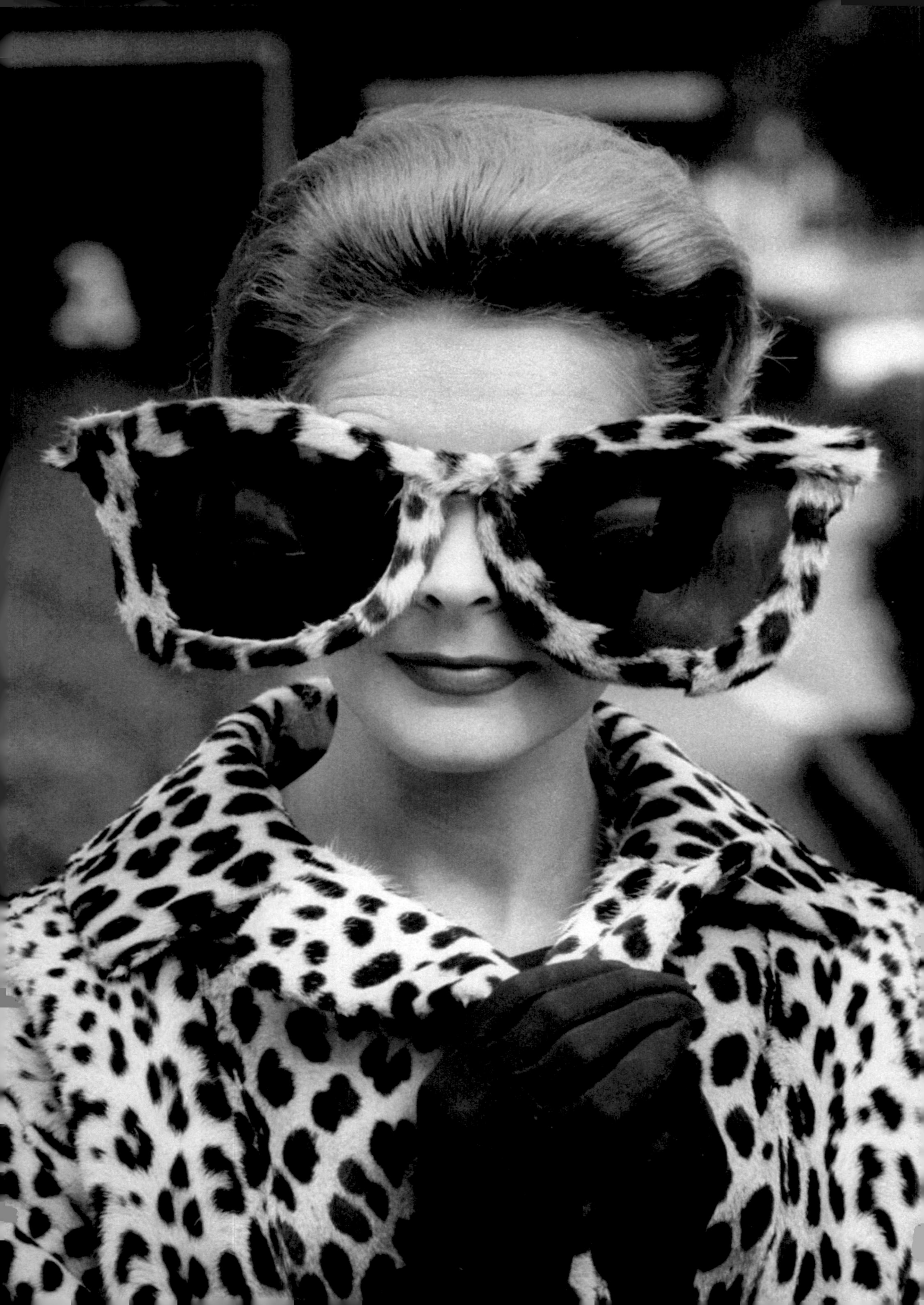

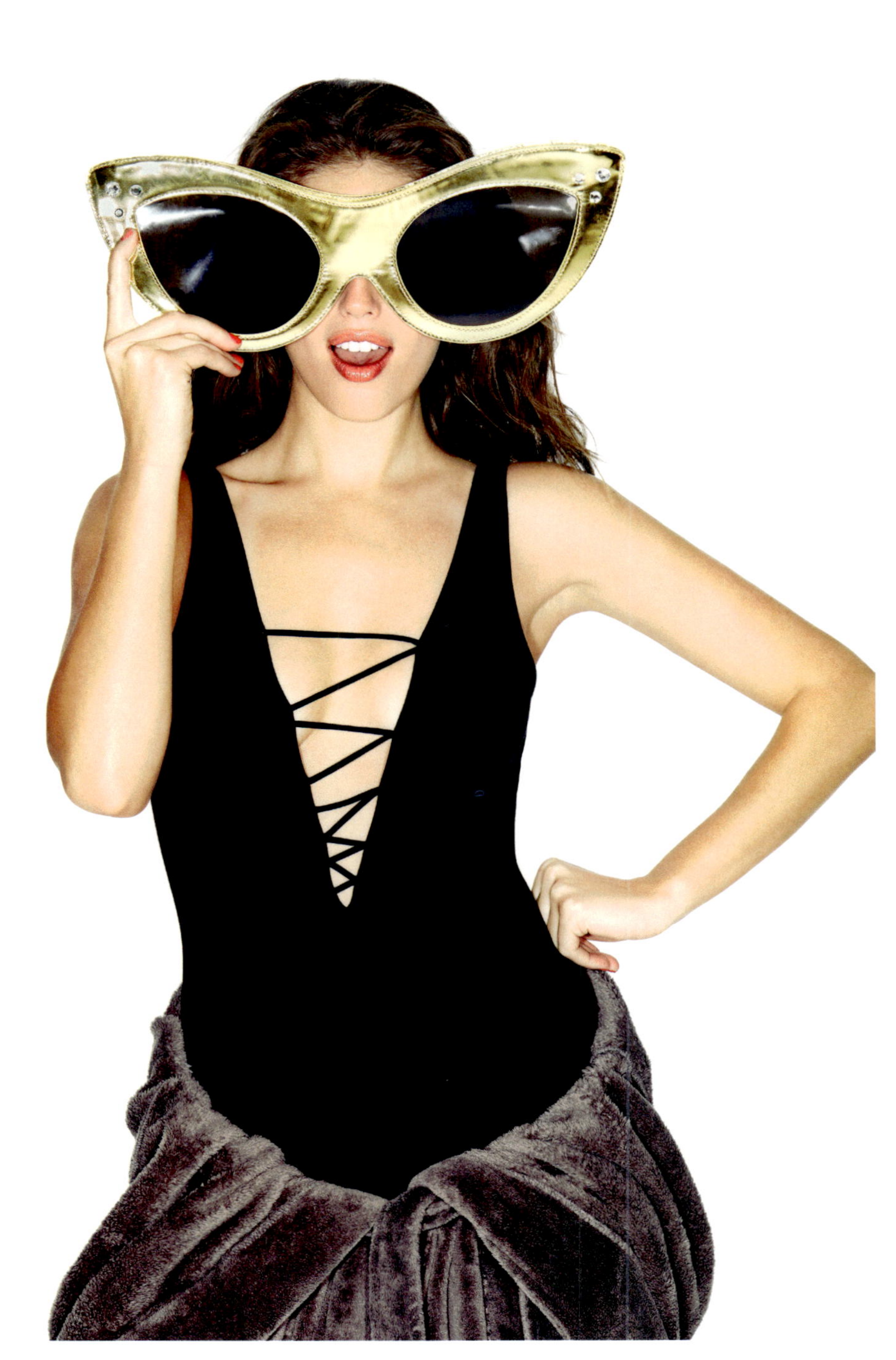

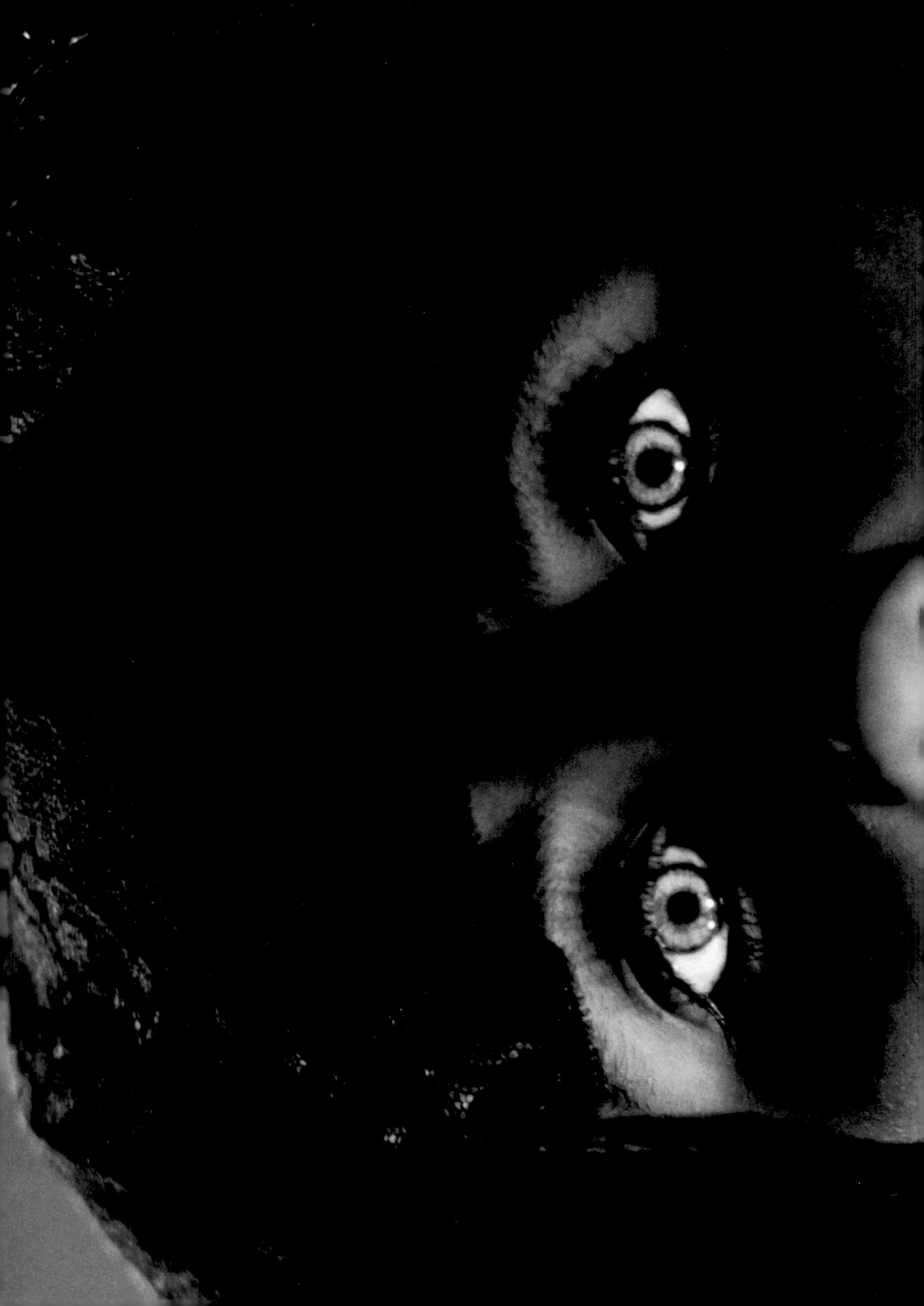

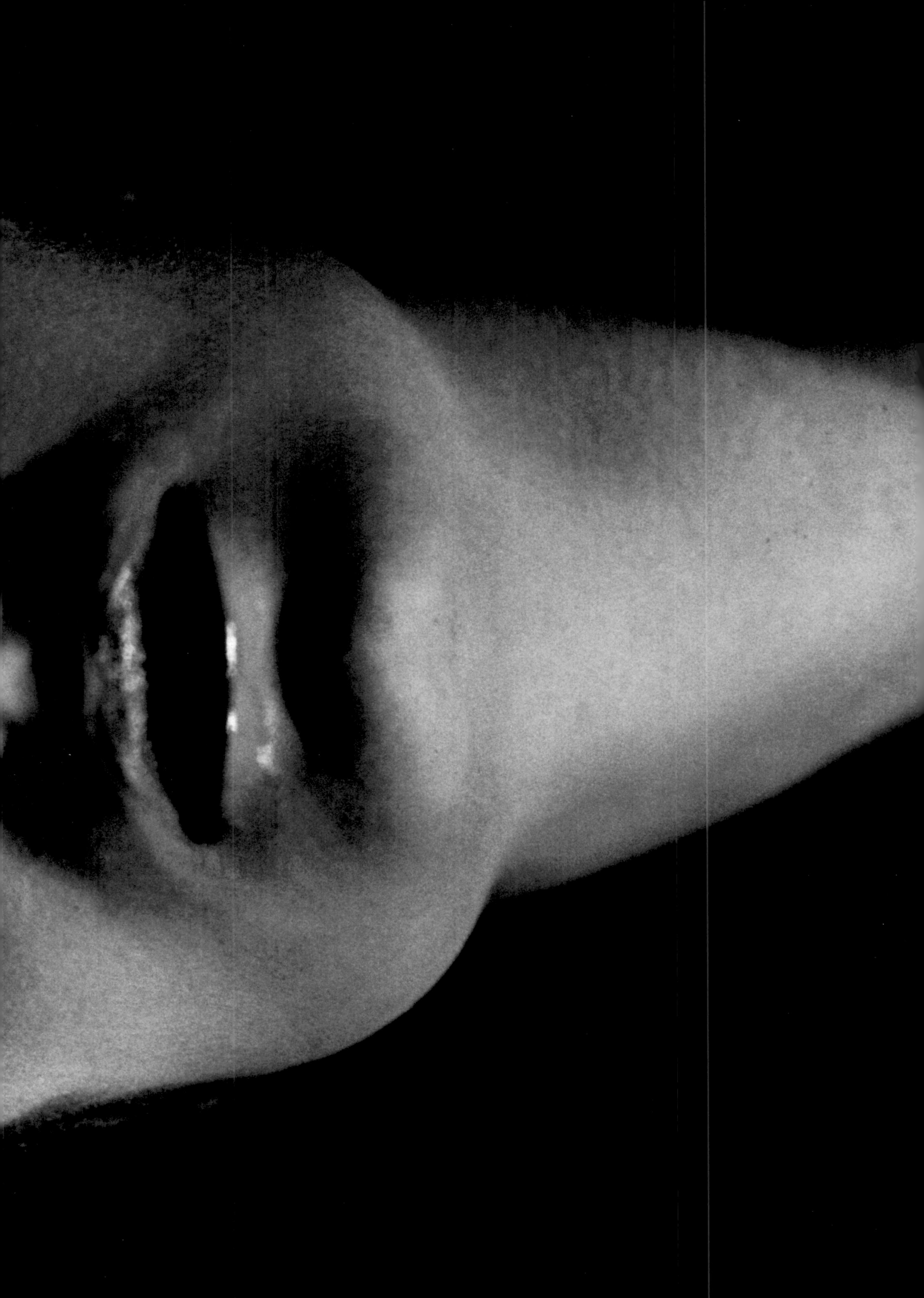

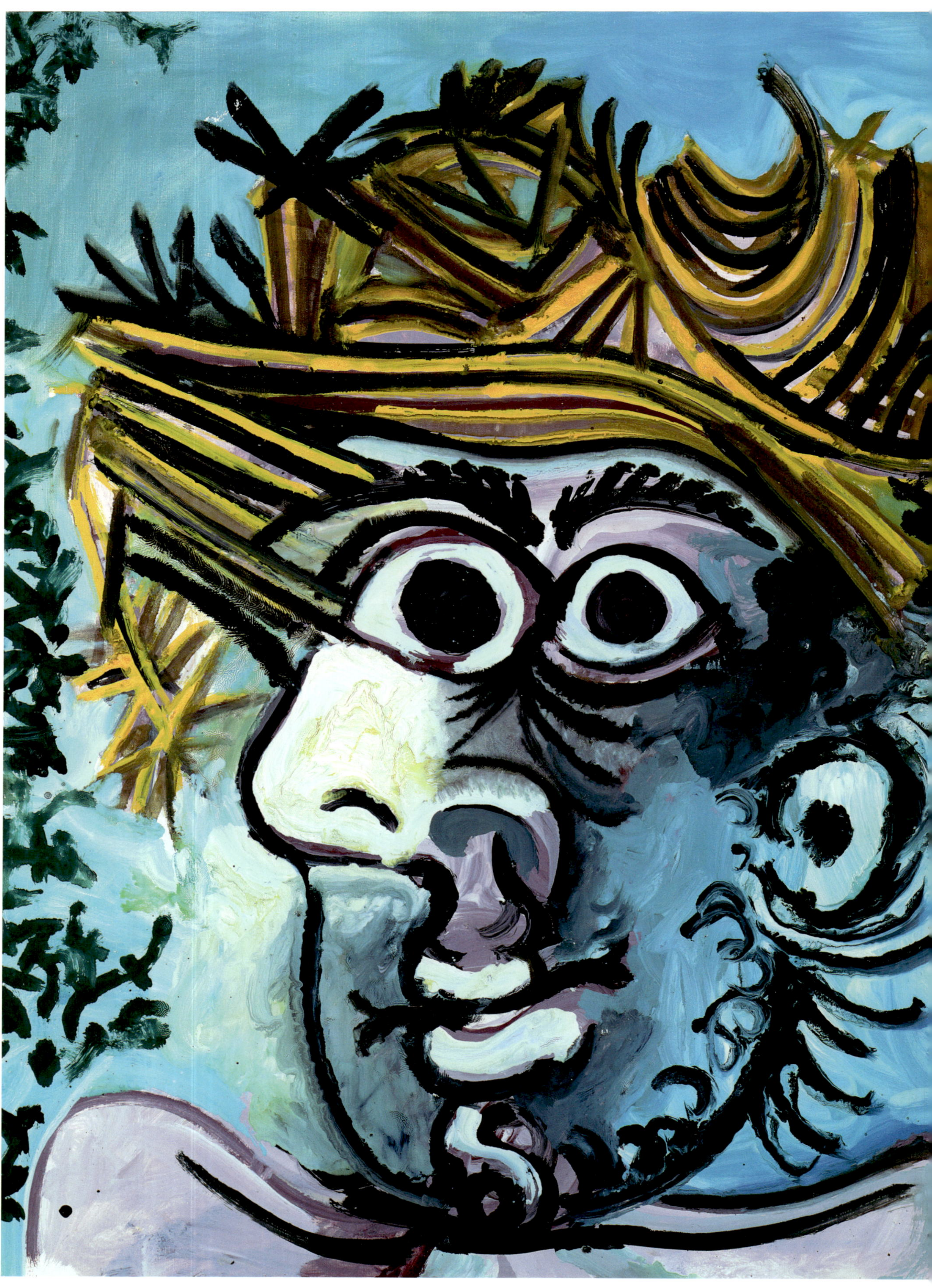

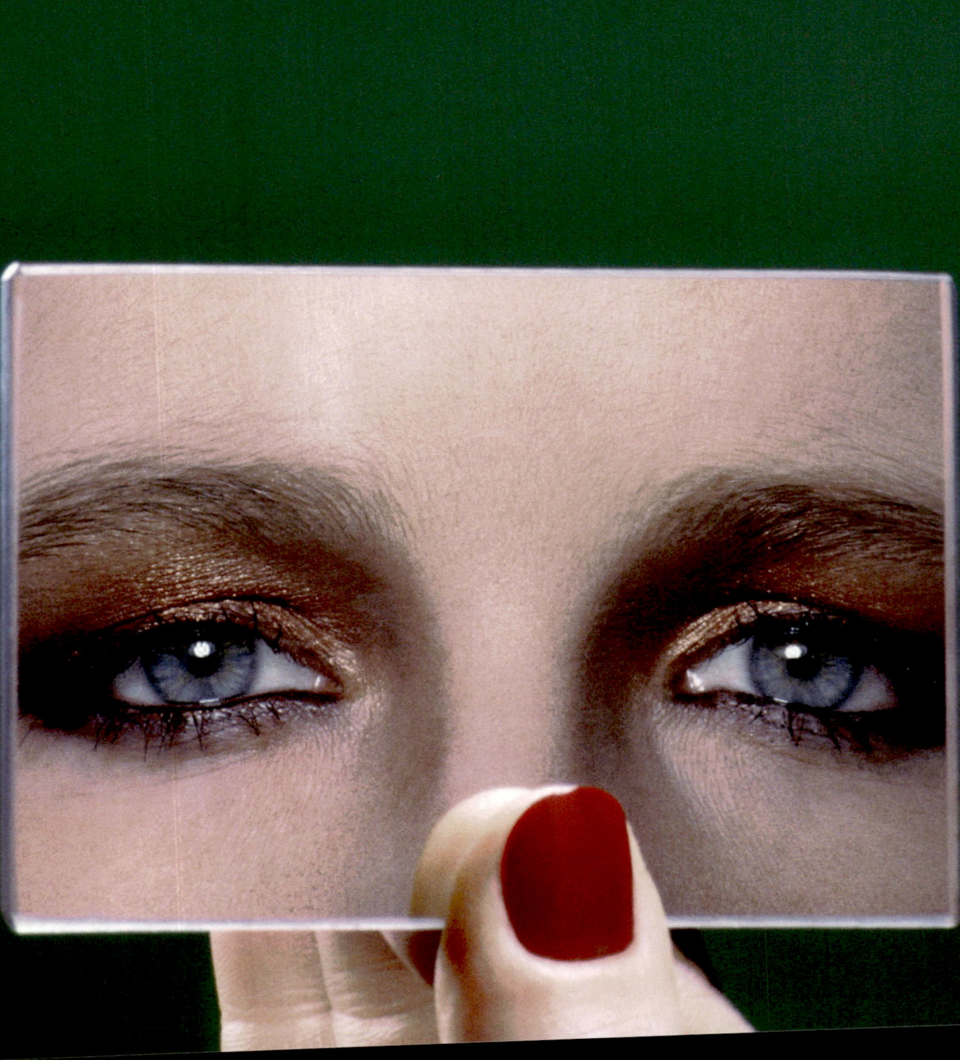

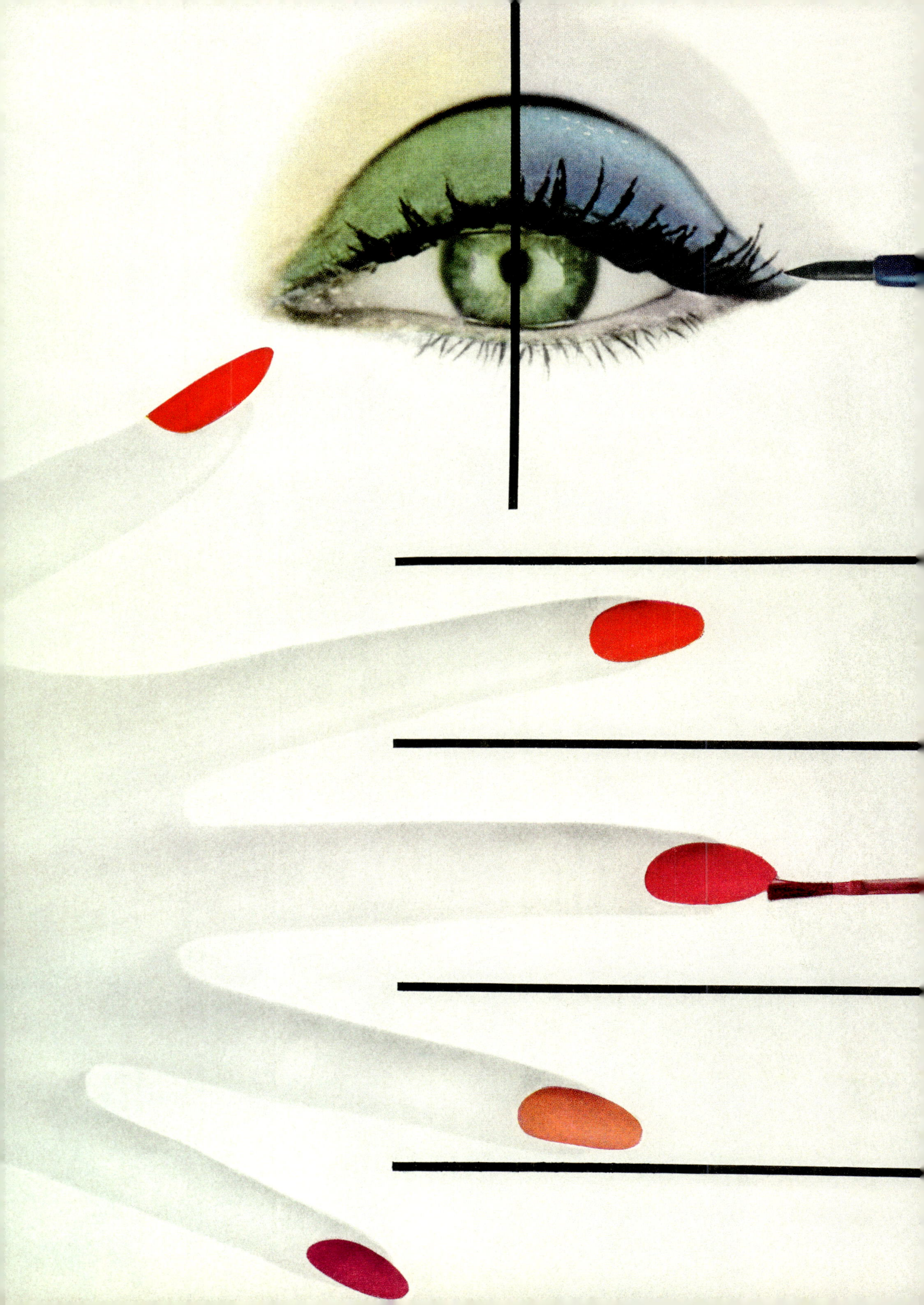

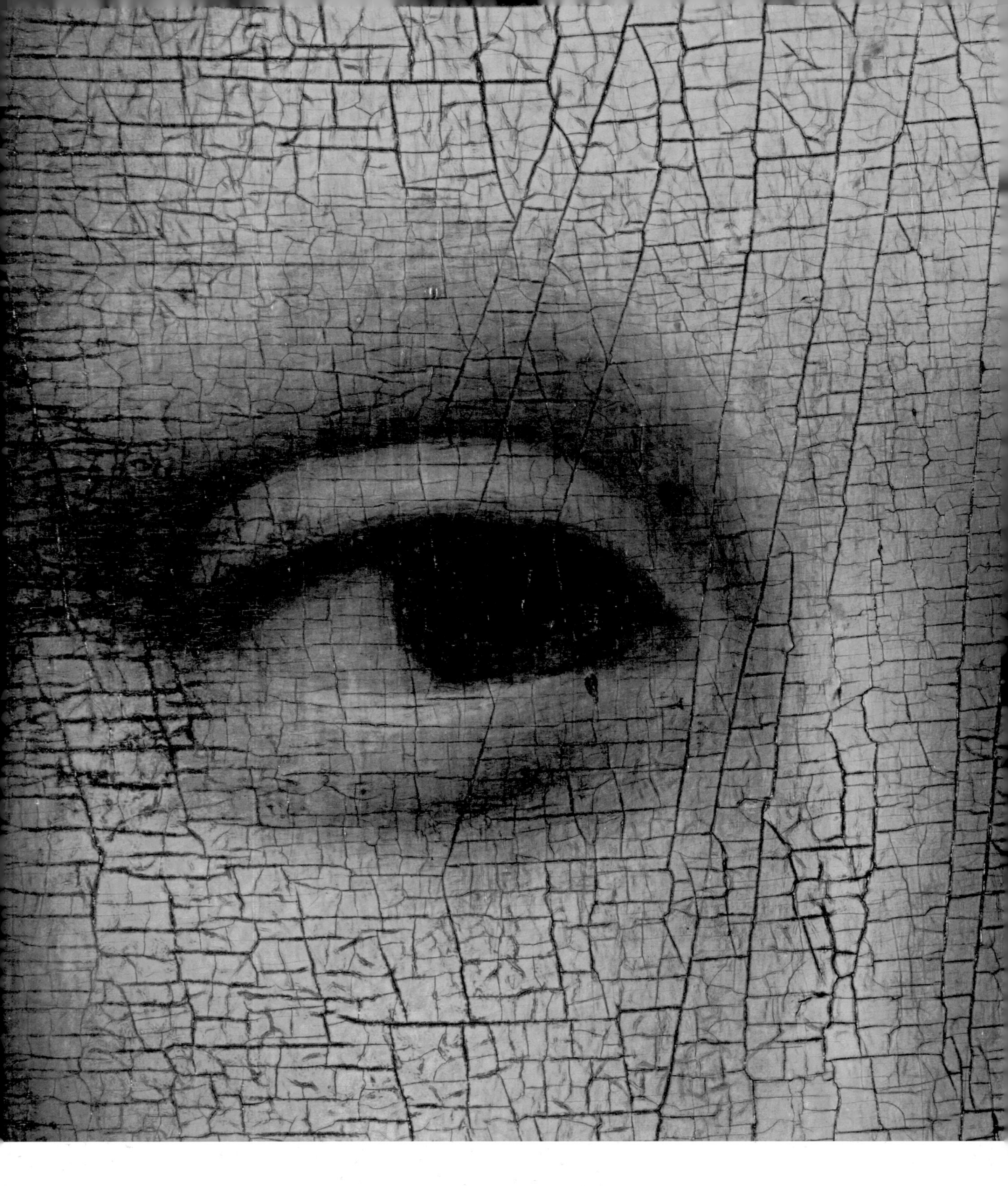

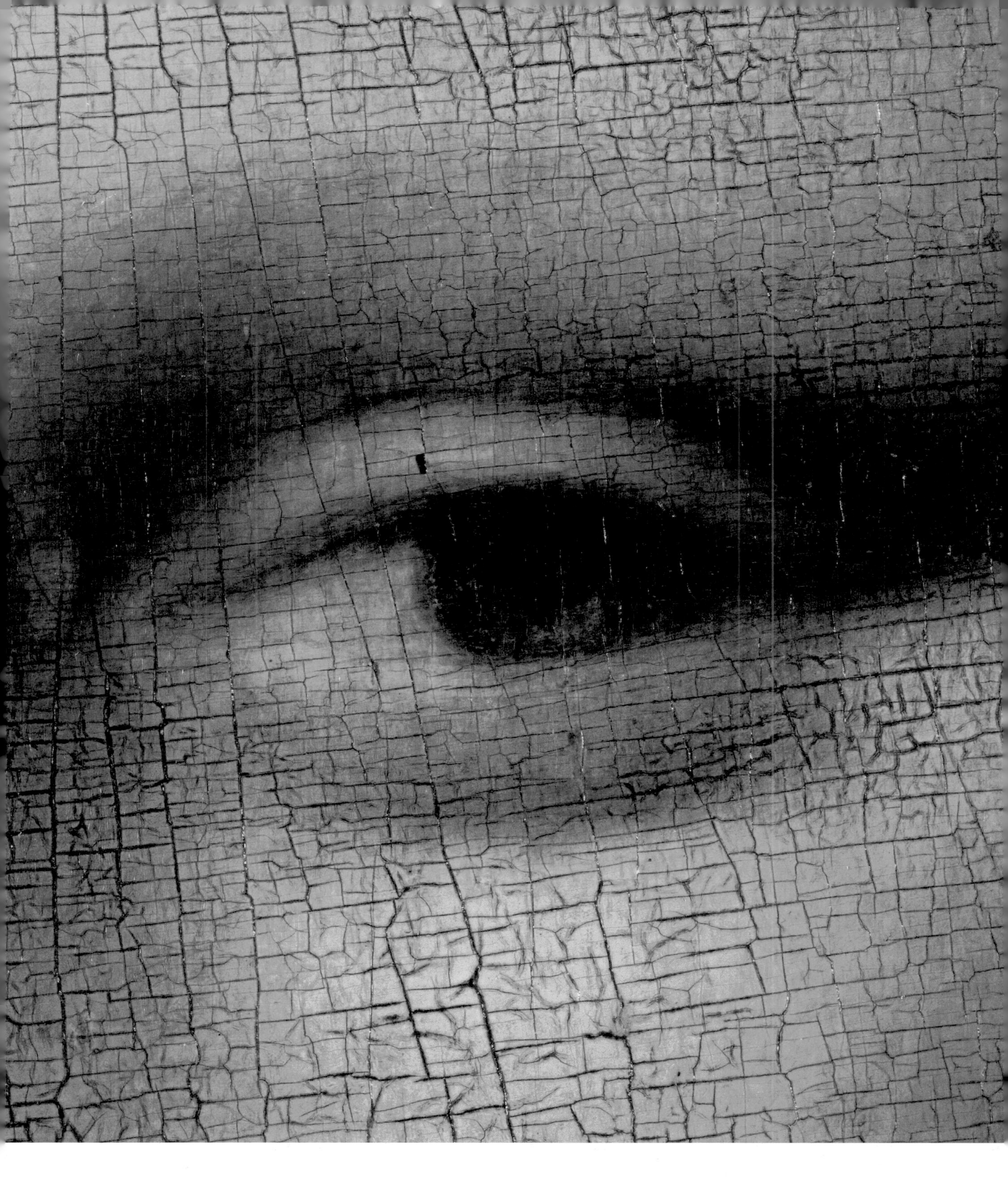

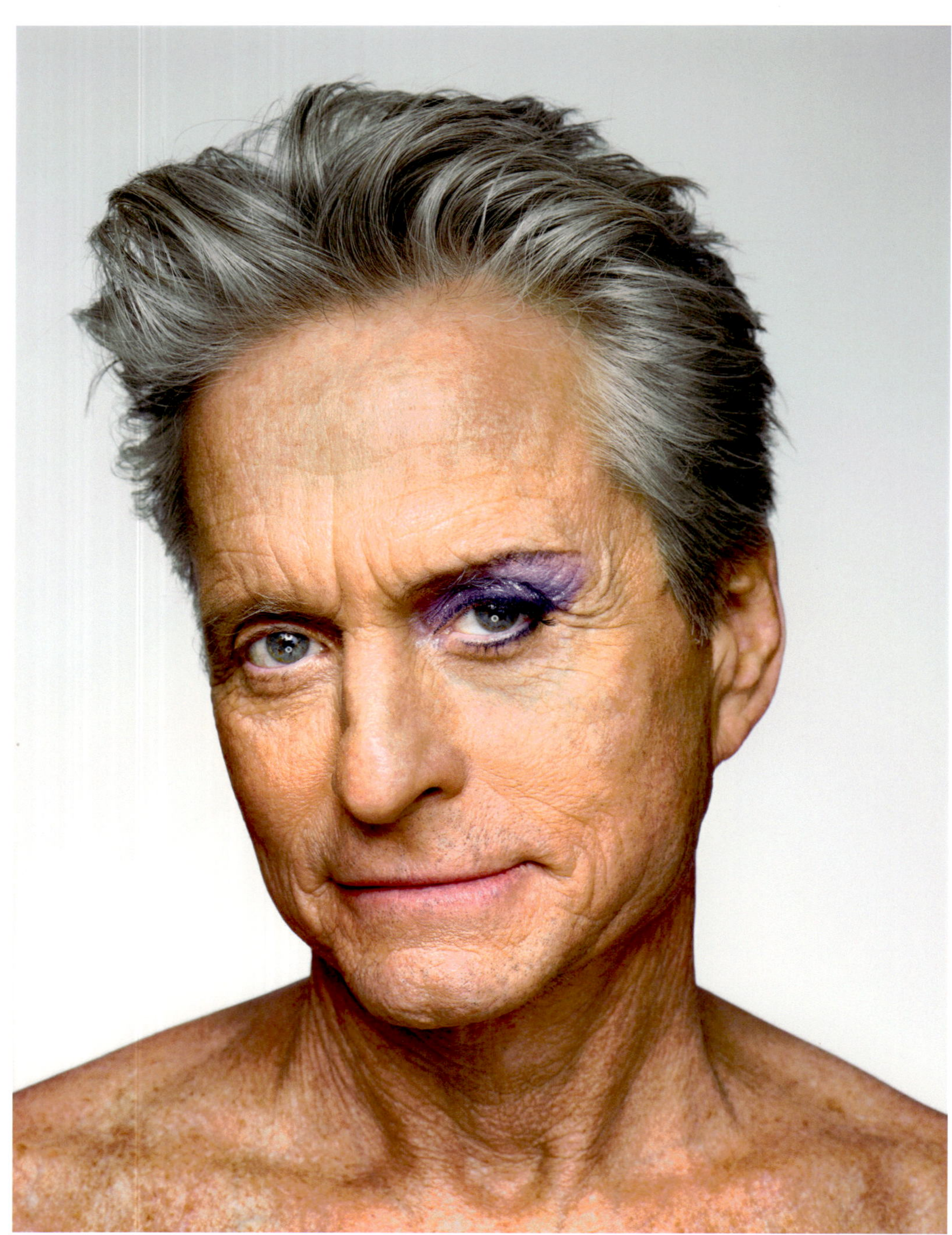

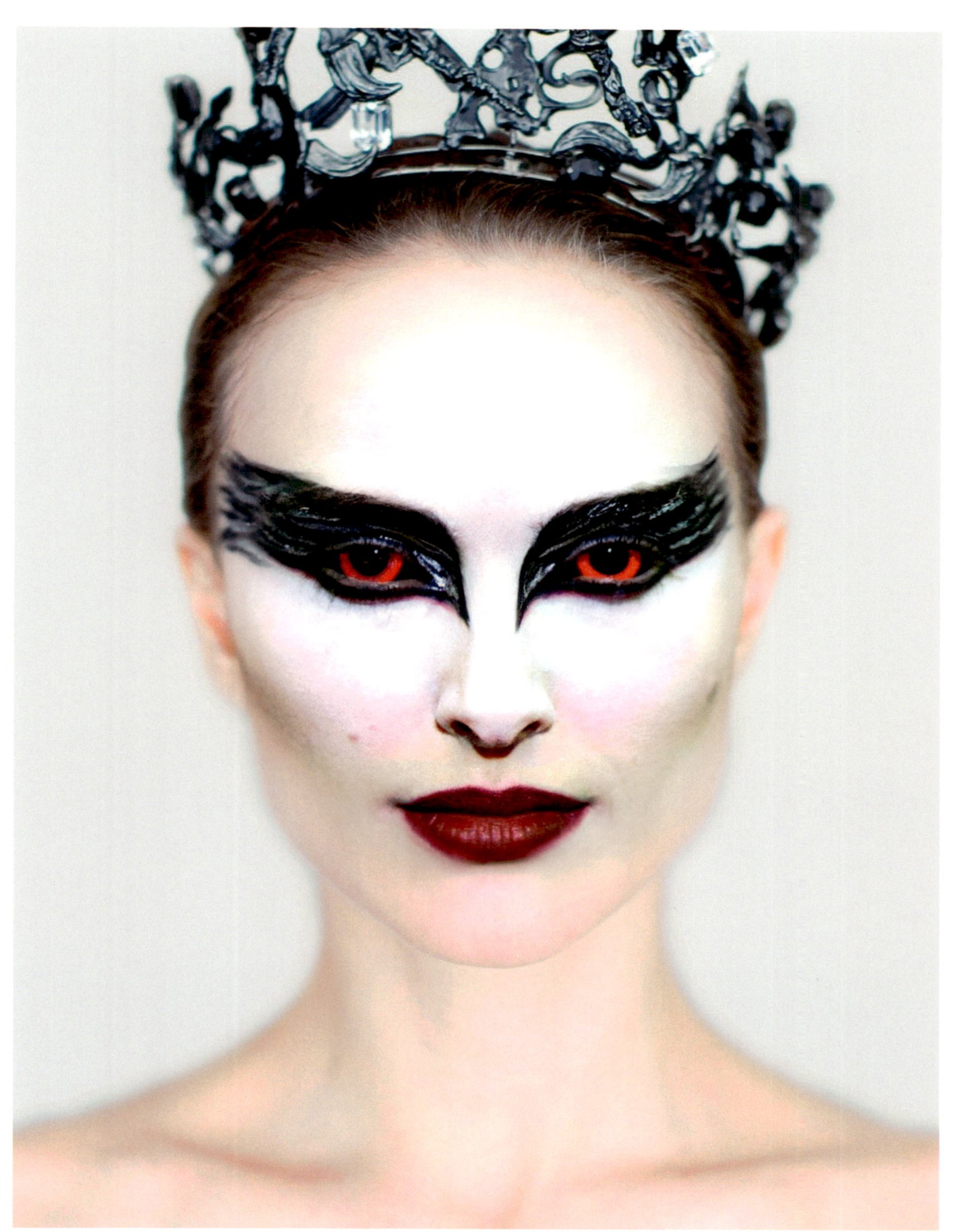

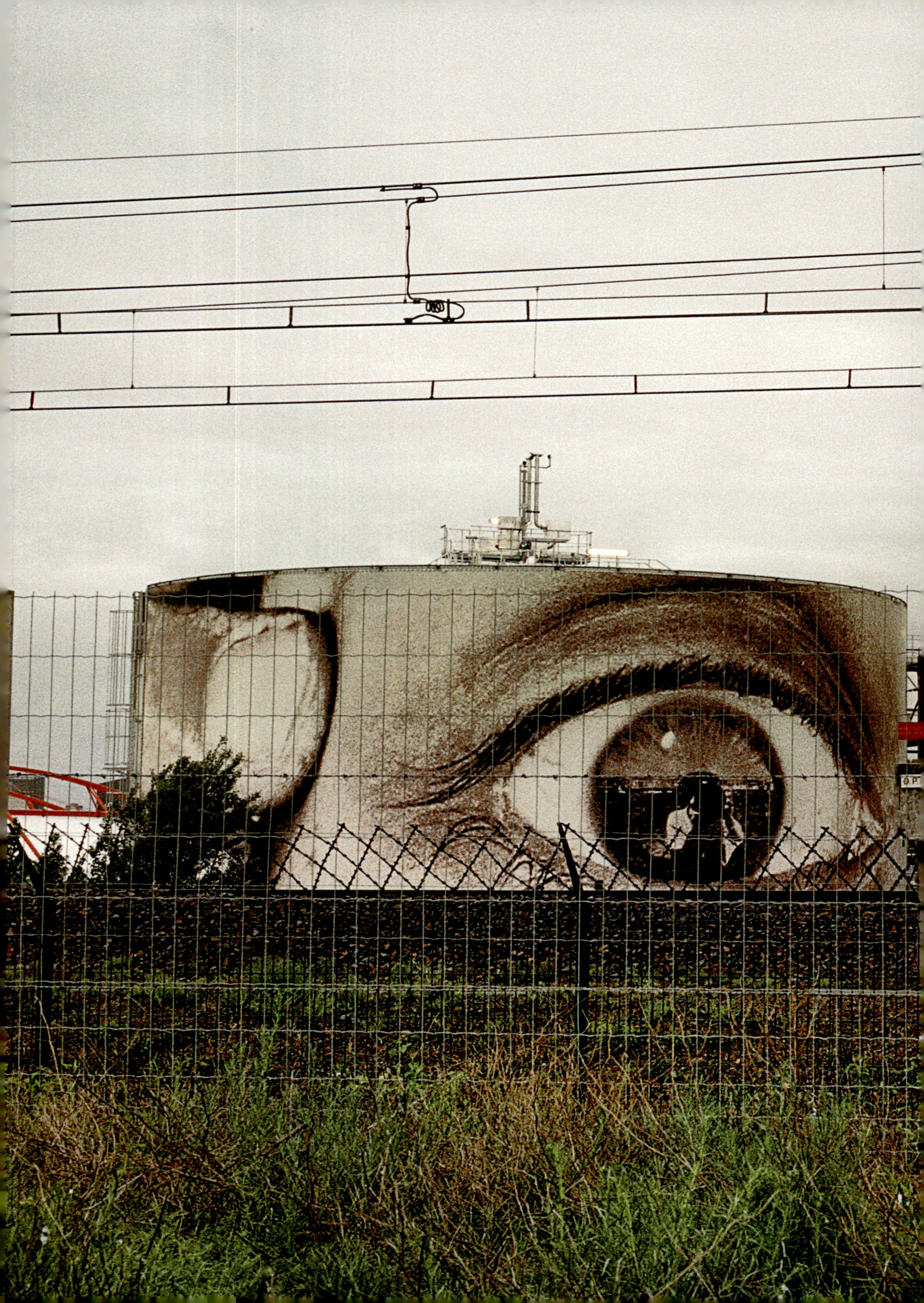

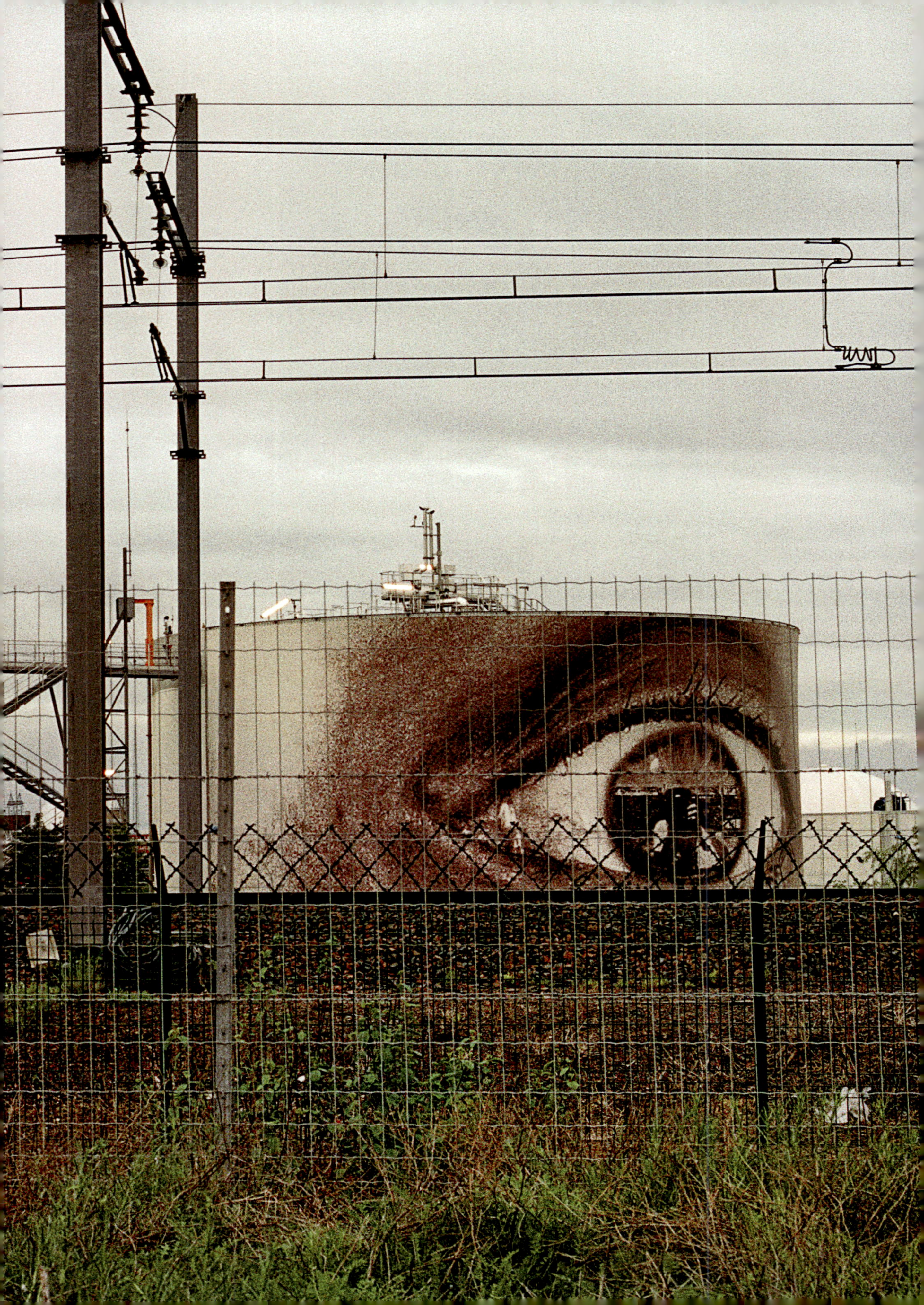

CBS

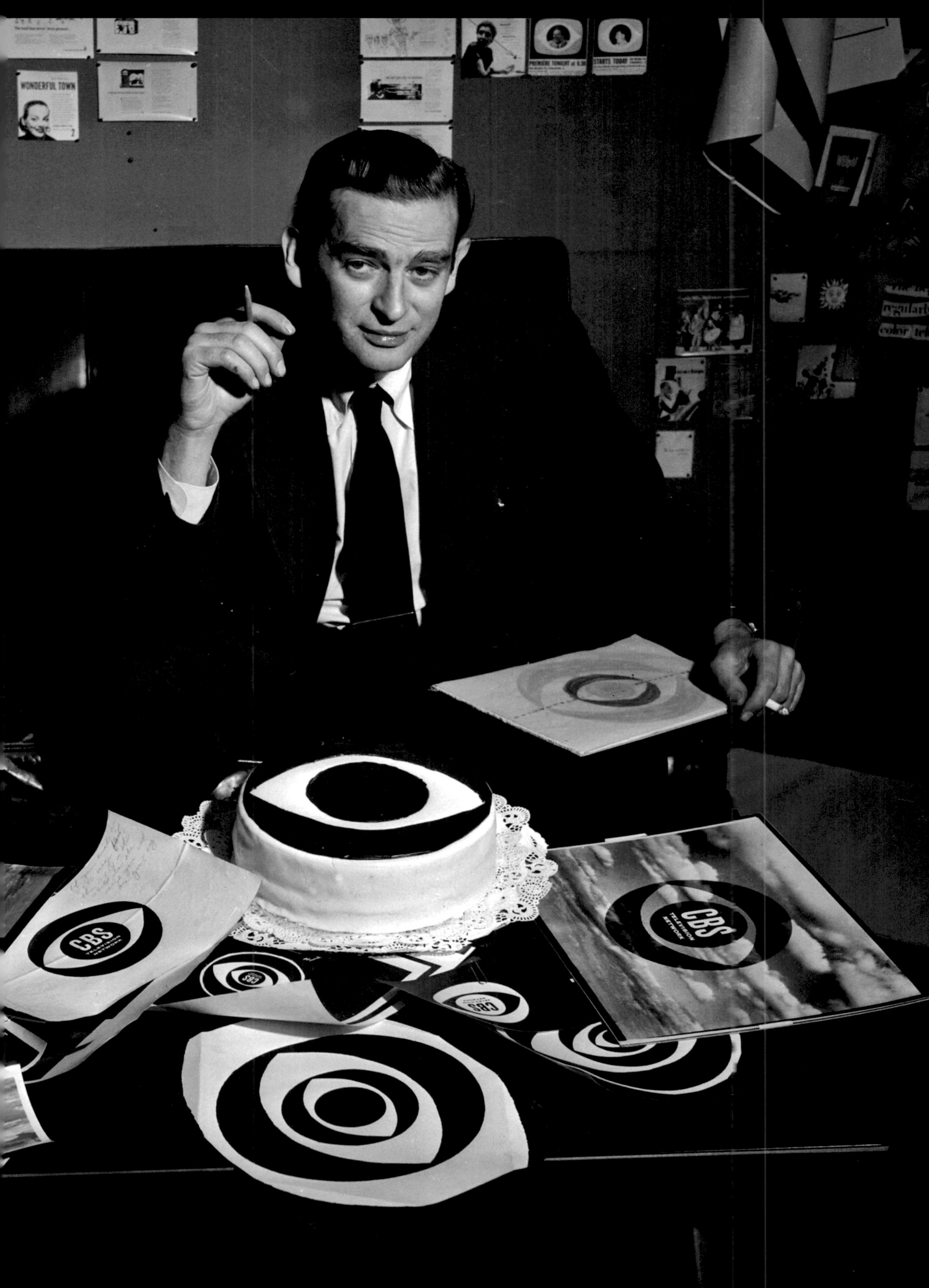
WONDERFUL TOWN
PREMIERE TONIGHT at 6:30
STARTS TODAY
CBS TELEVISION NETWORK
CBS TELEVISION NETWORK

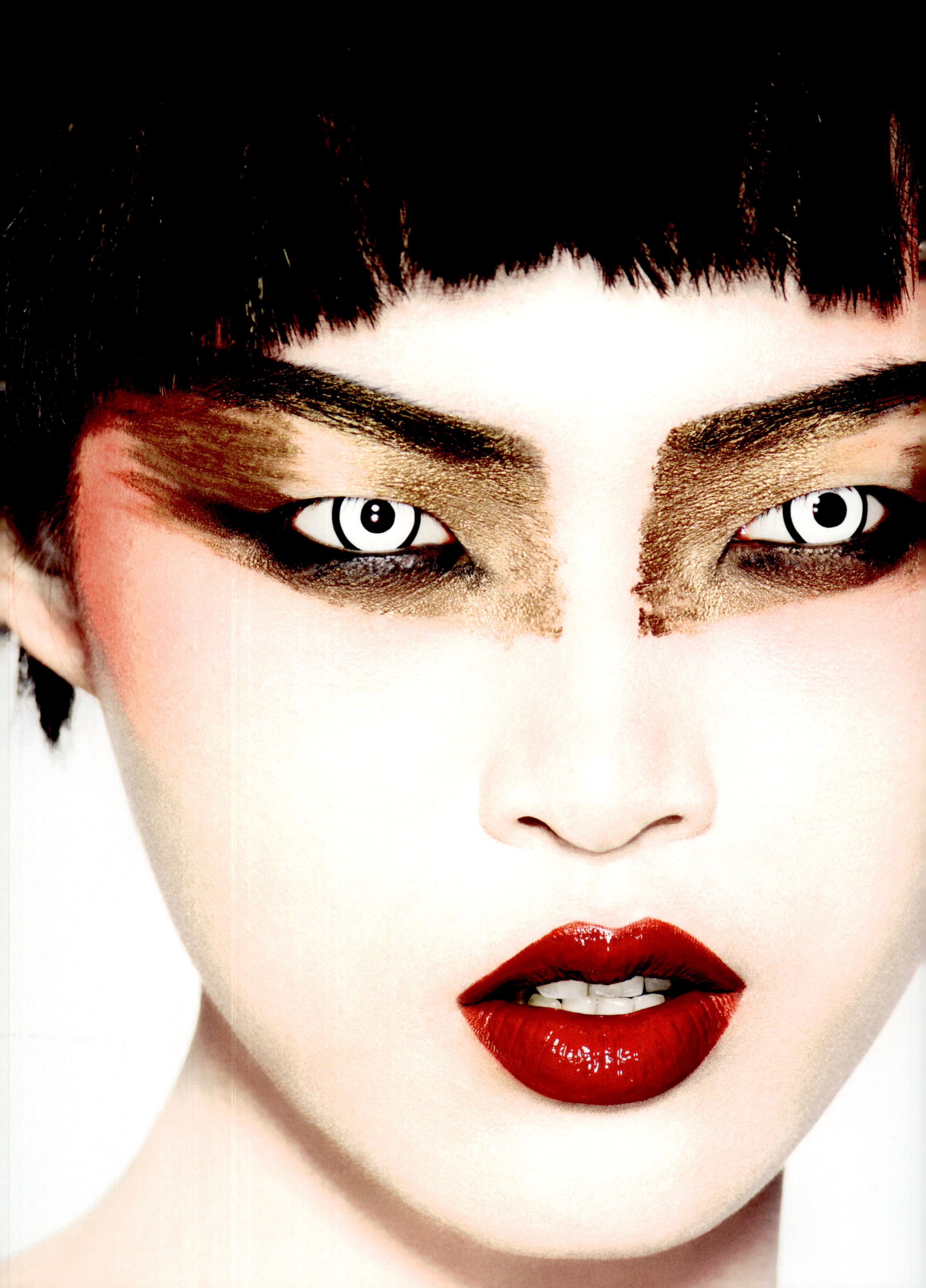

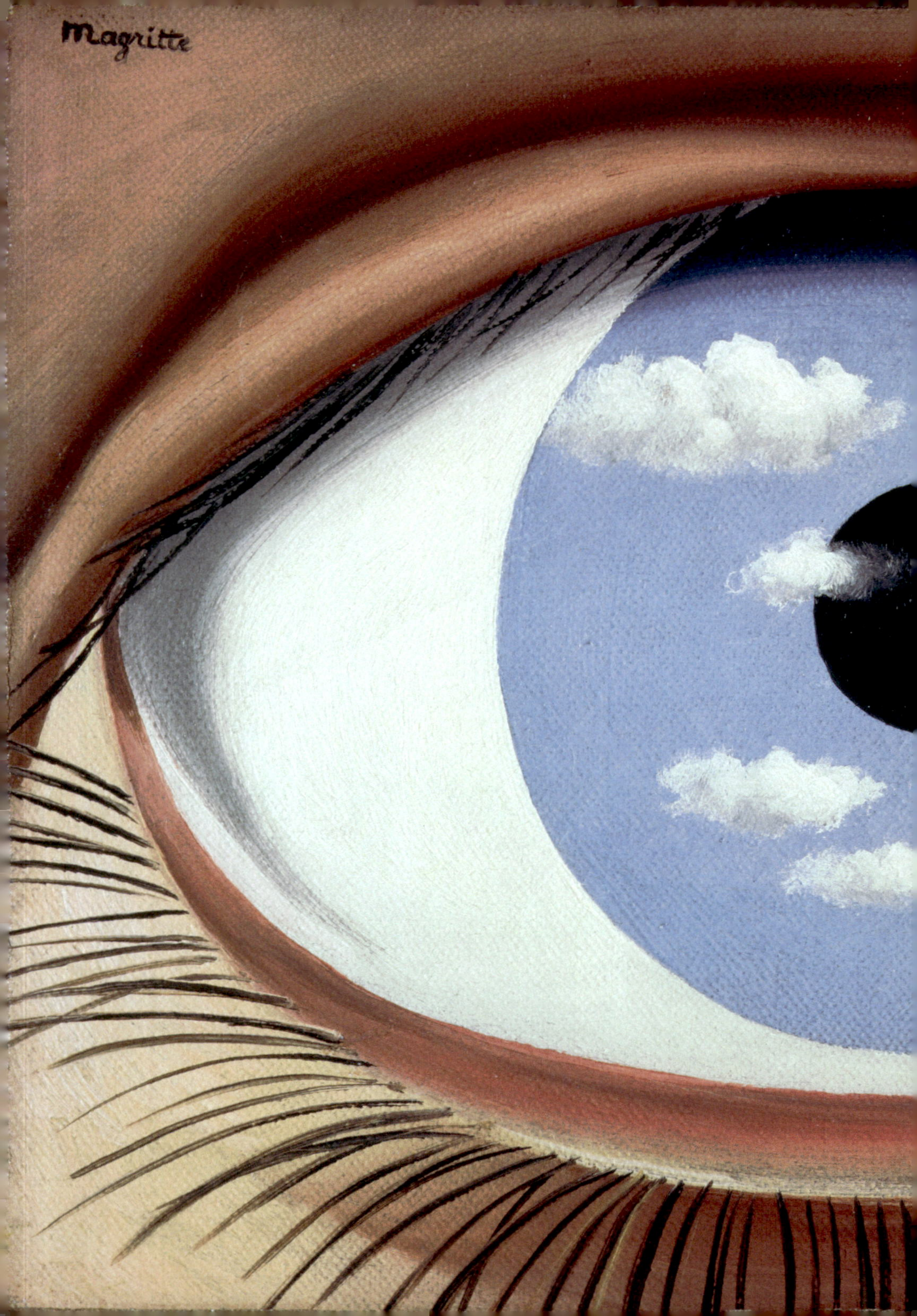
Magritte

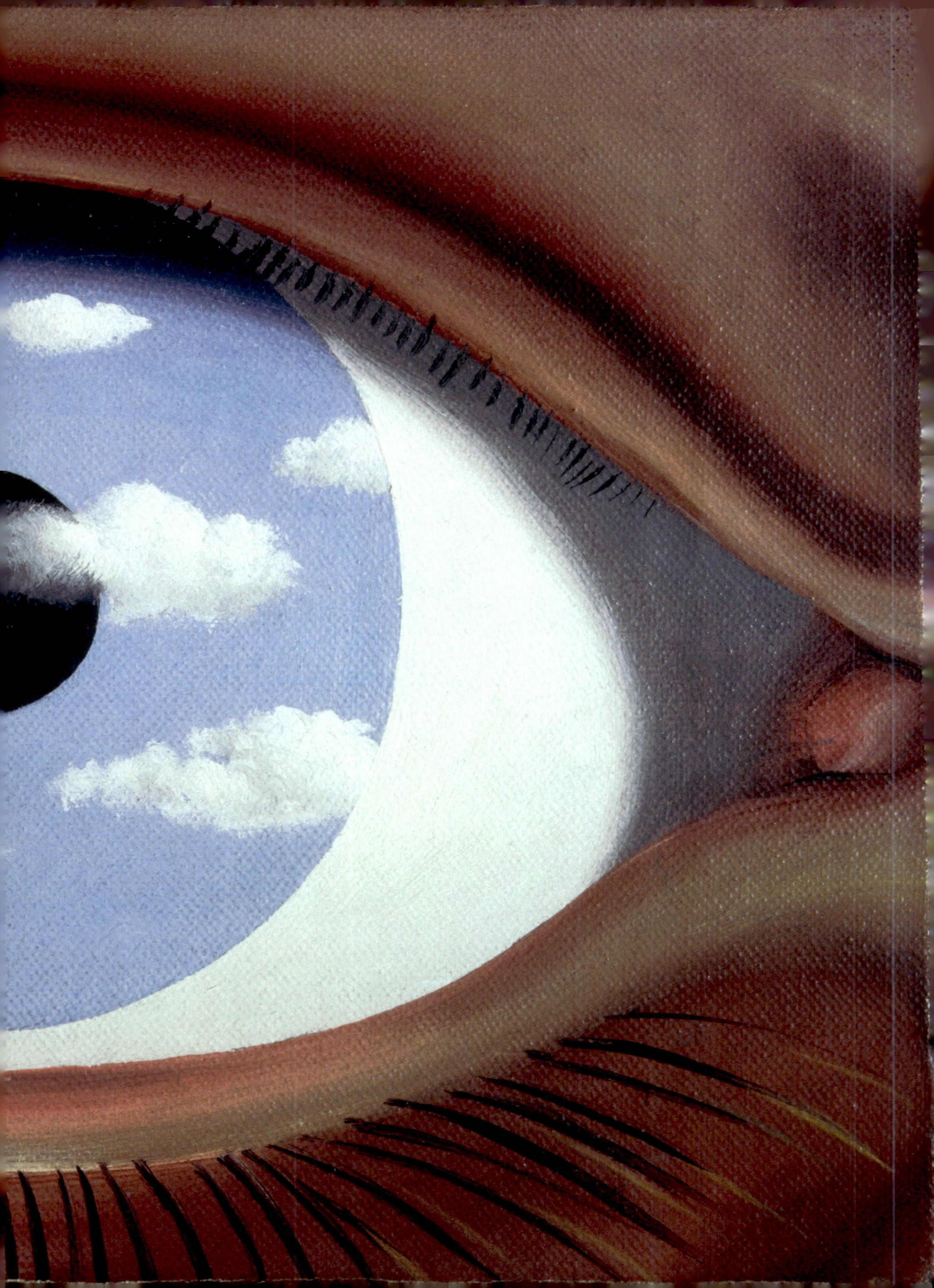

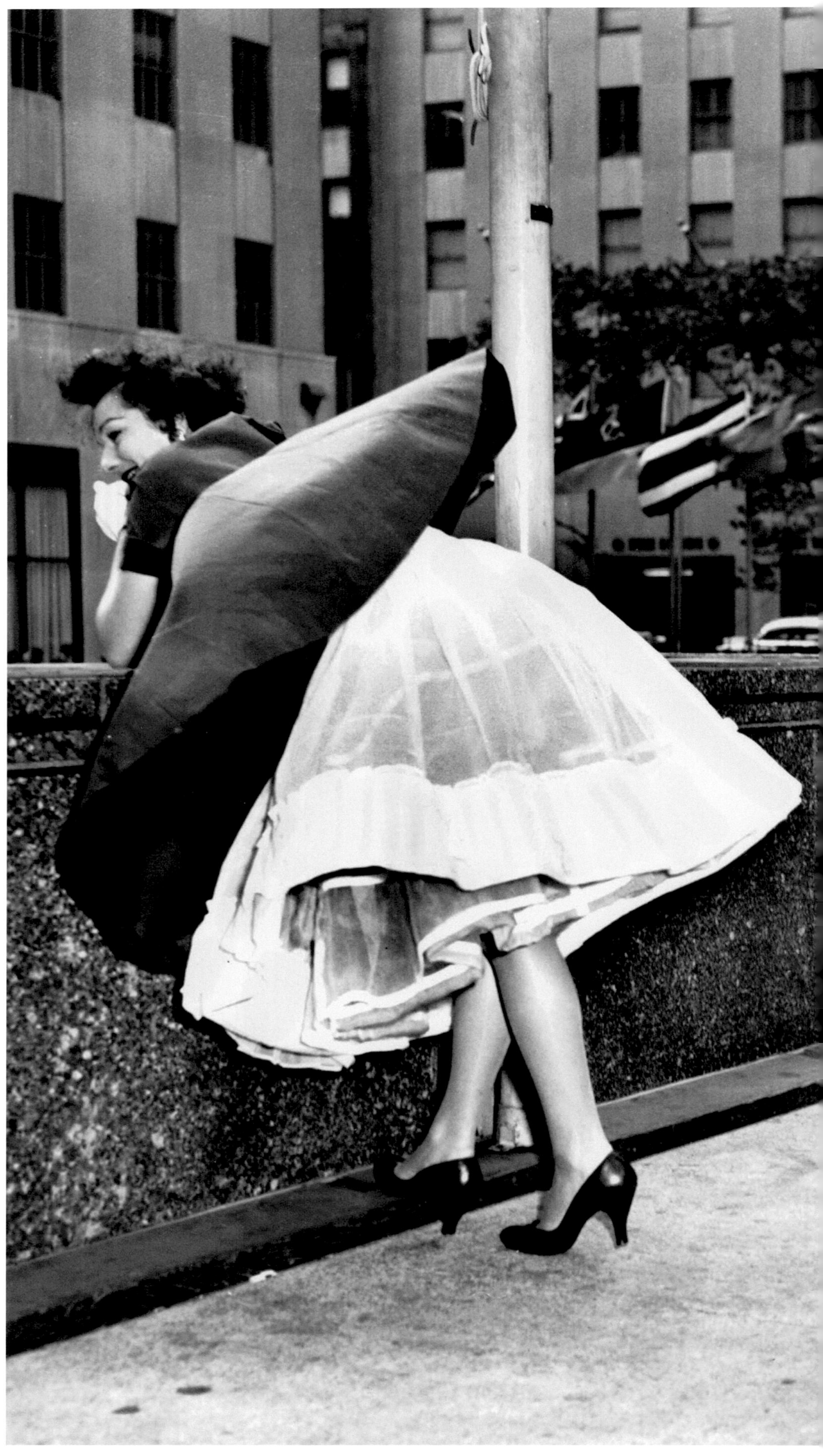

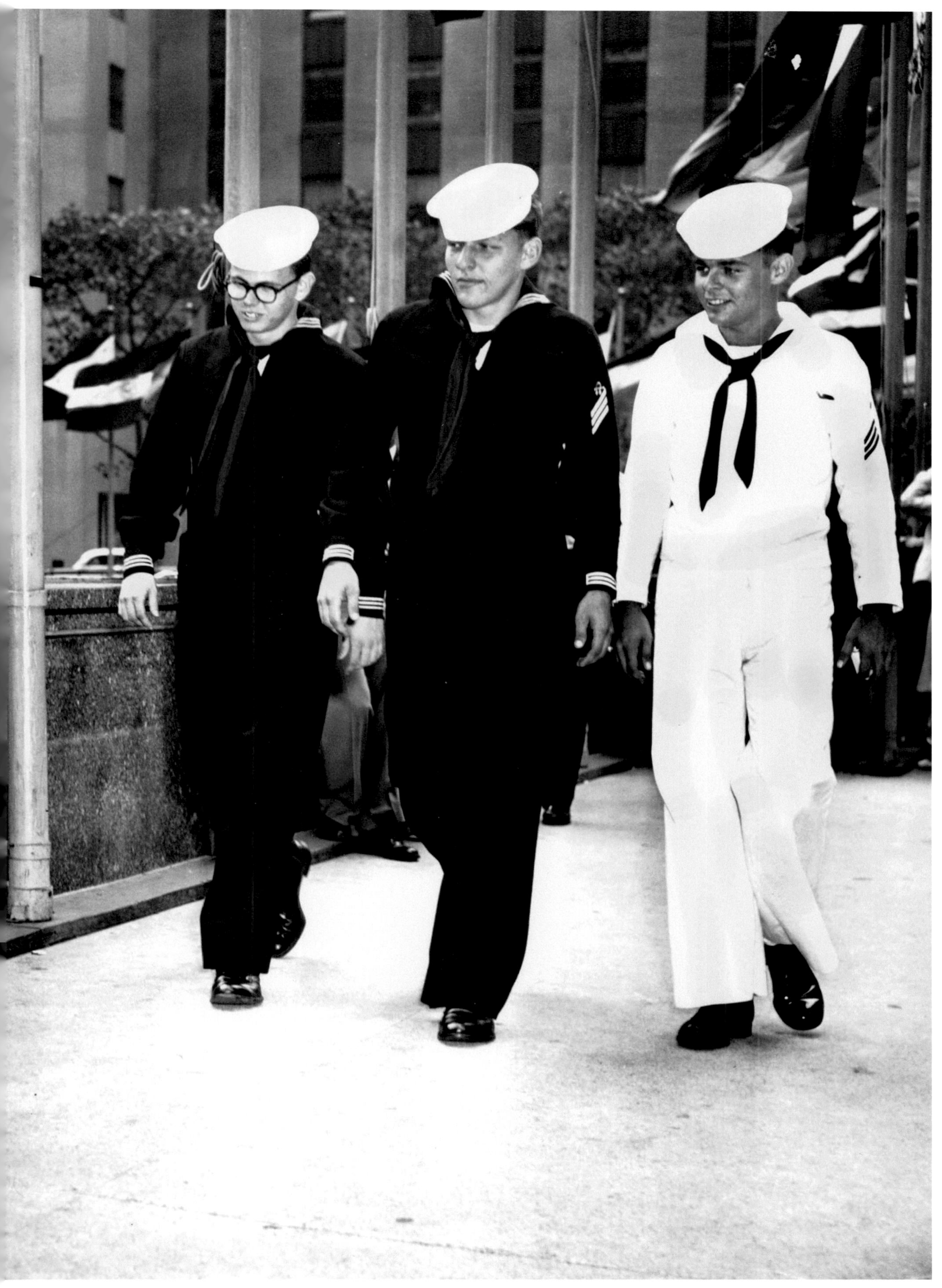

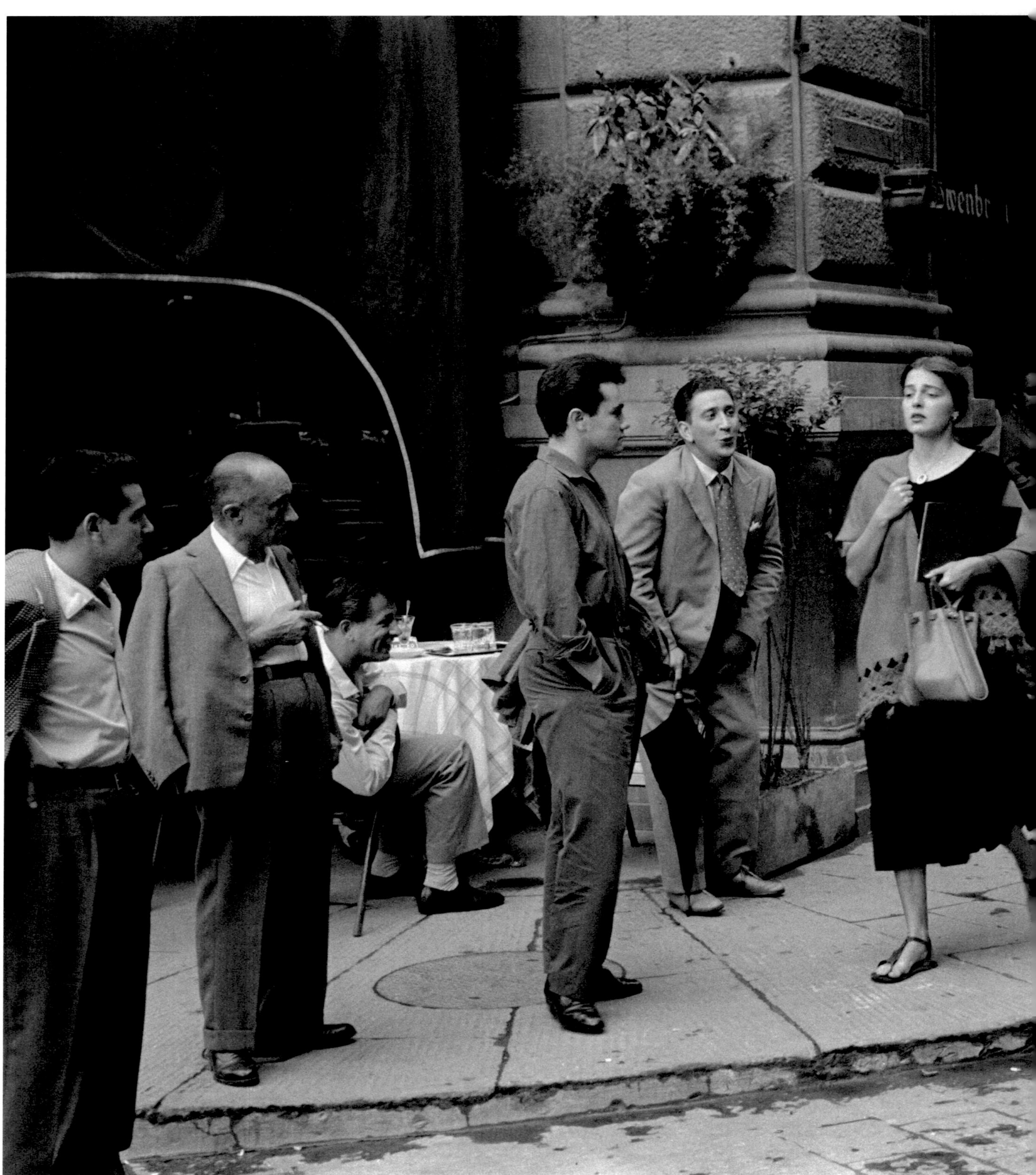

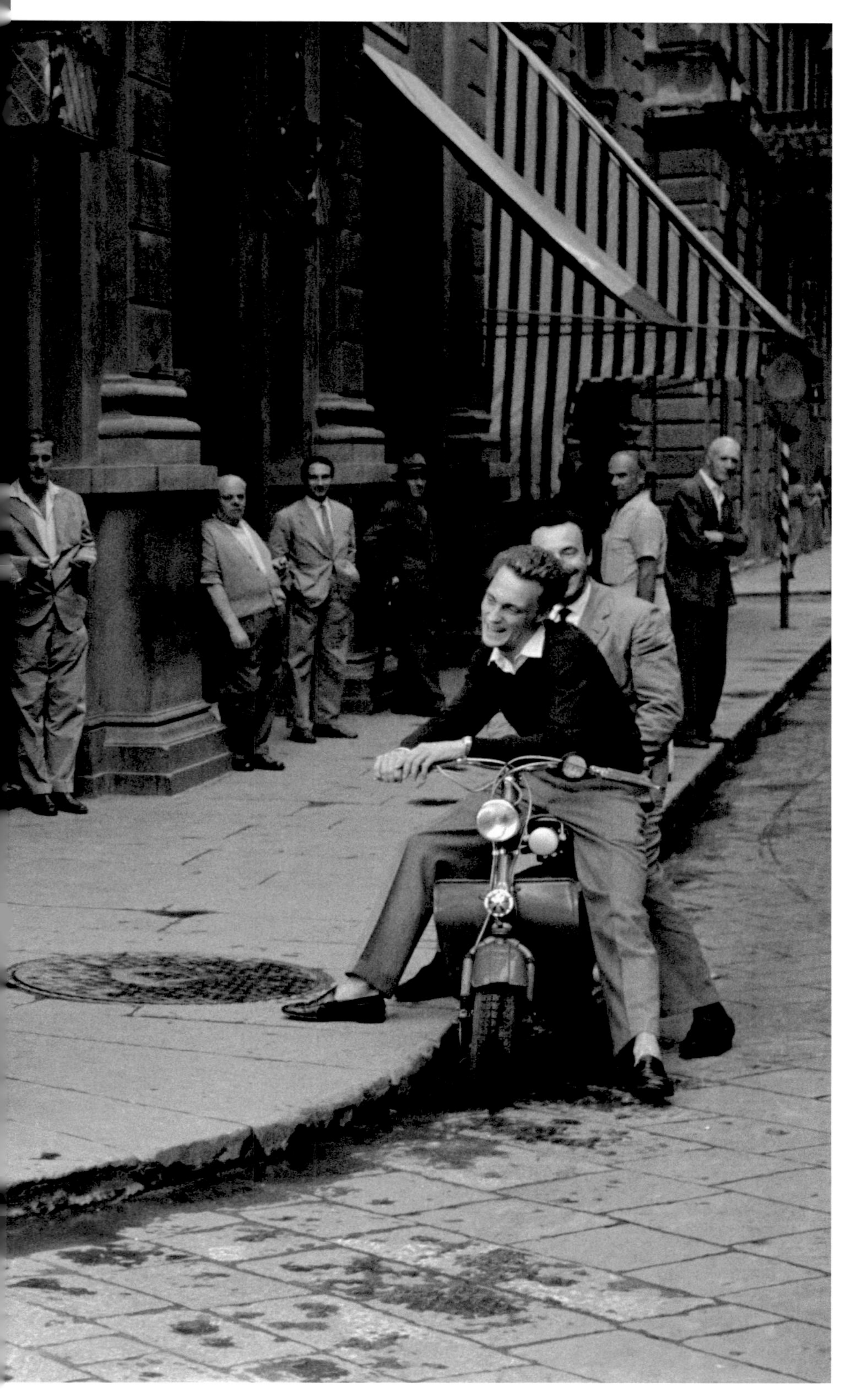

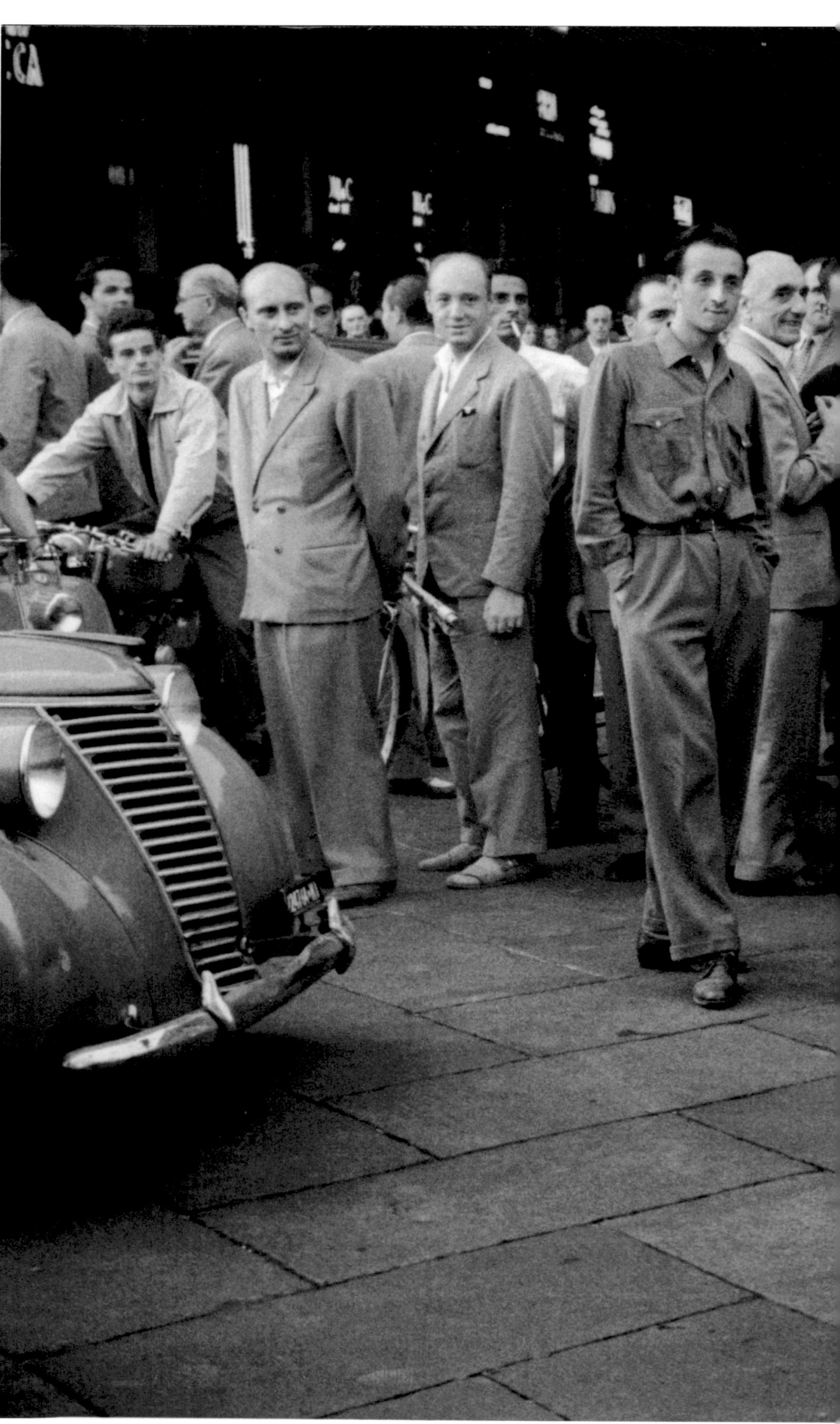

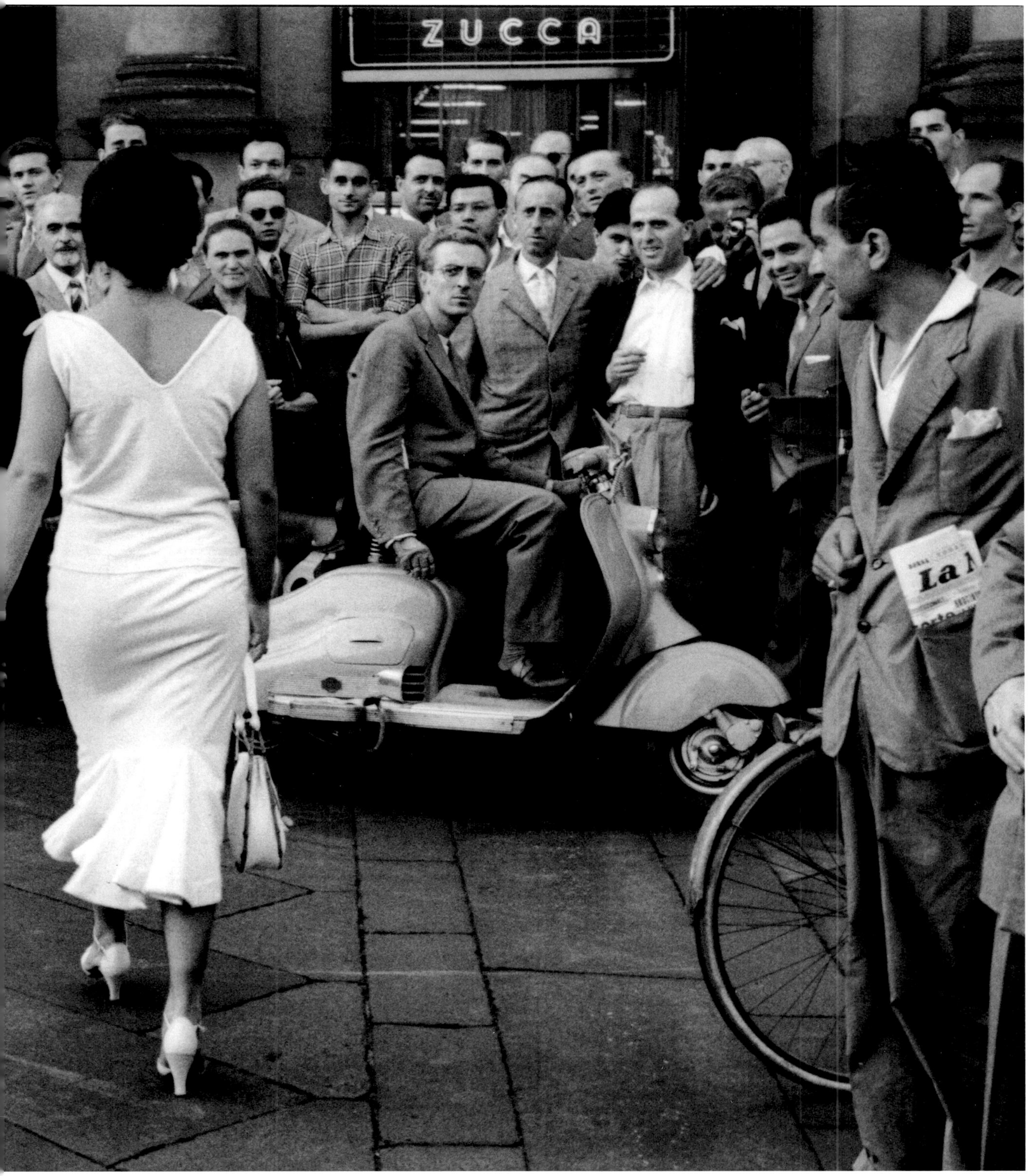

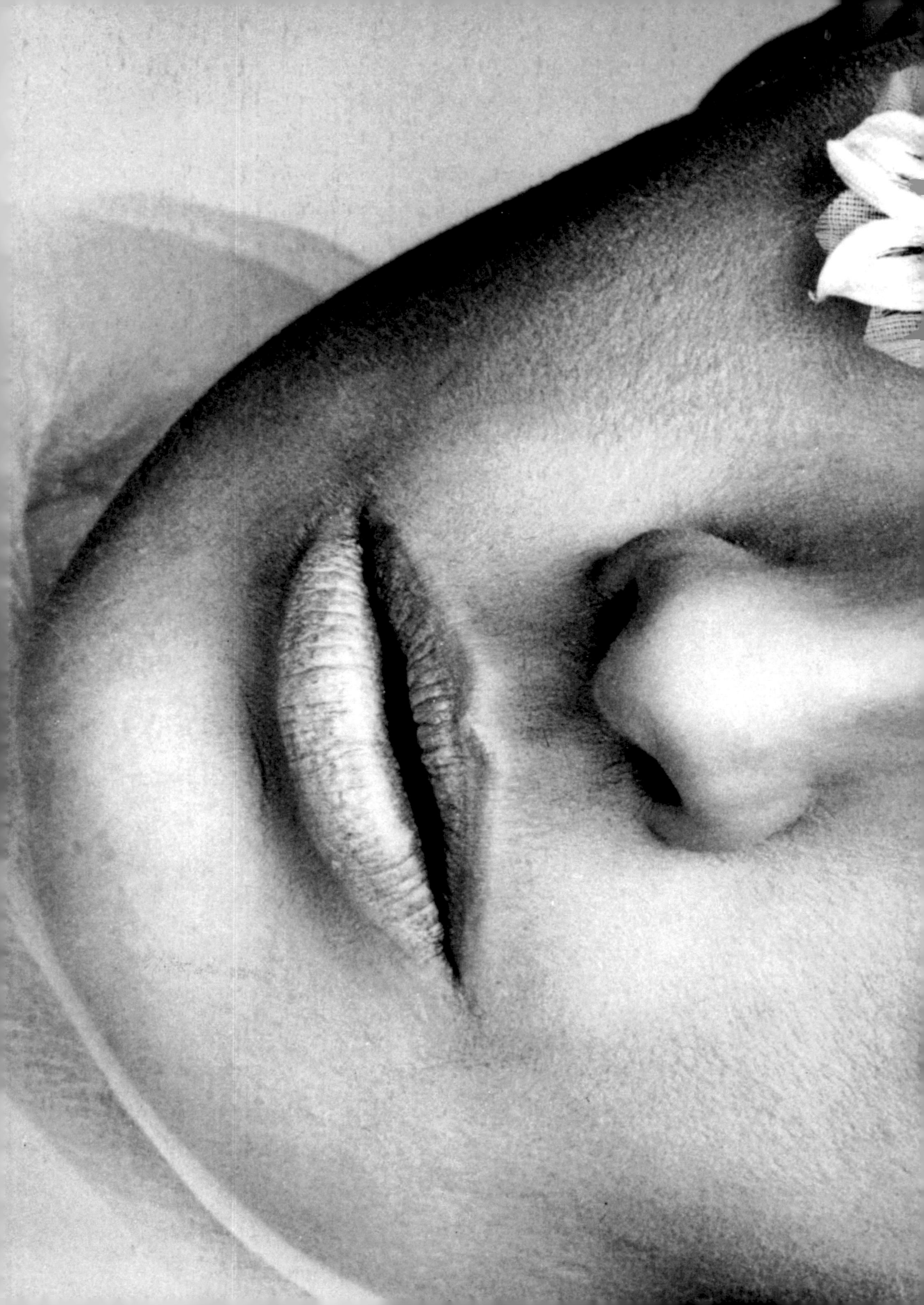

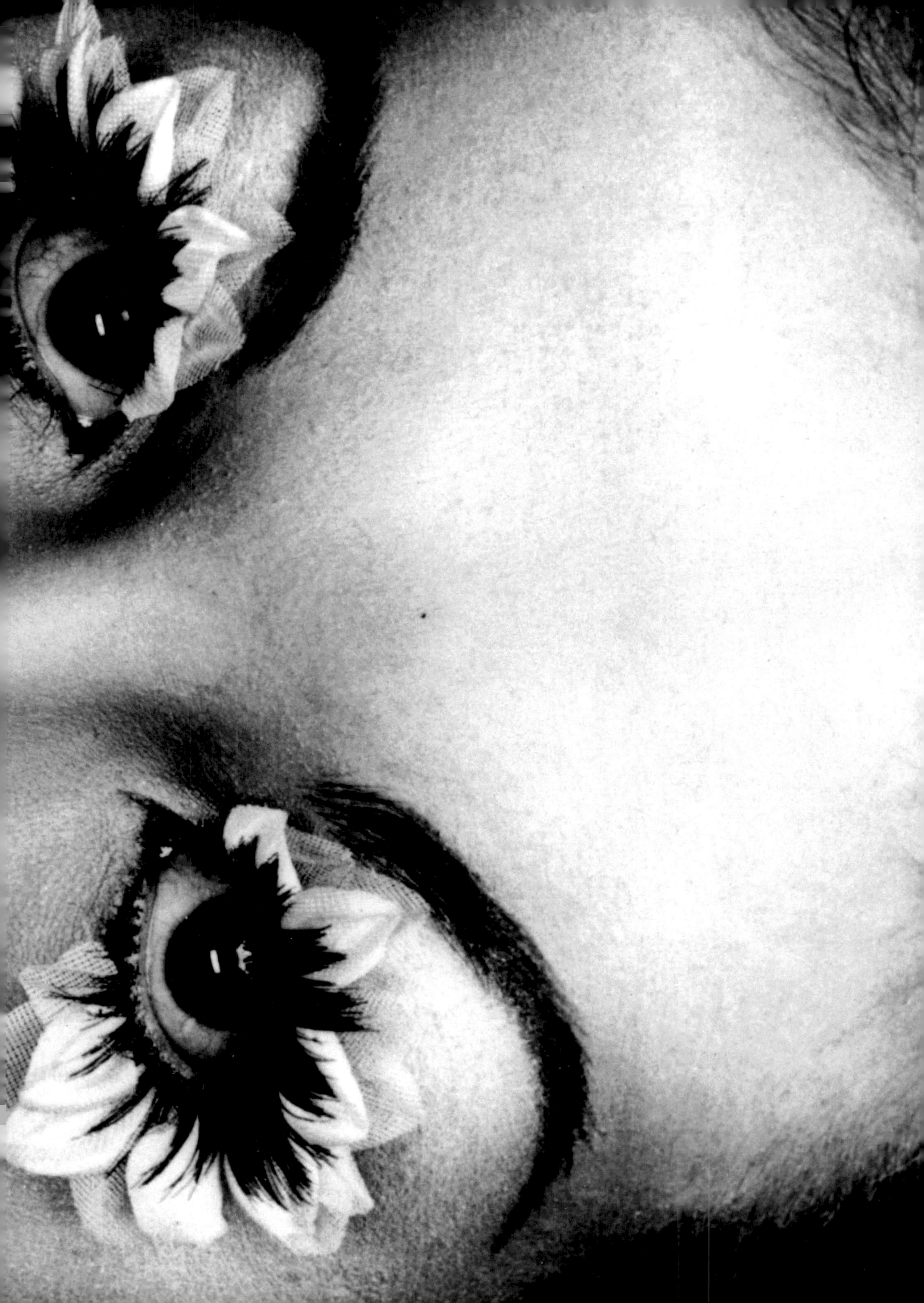

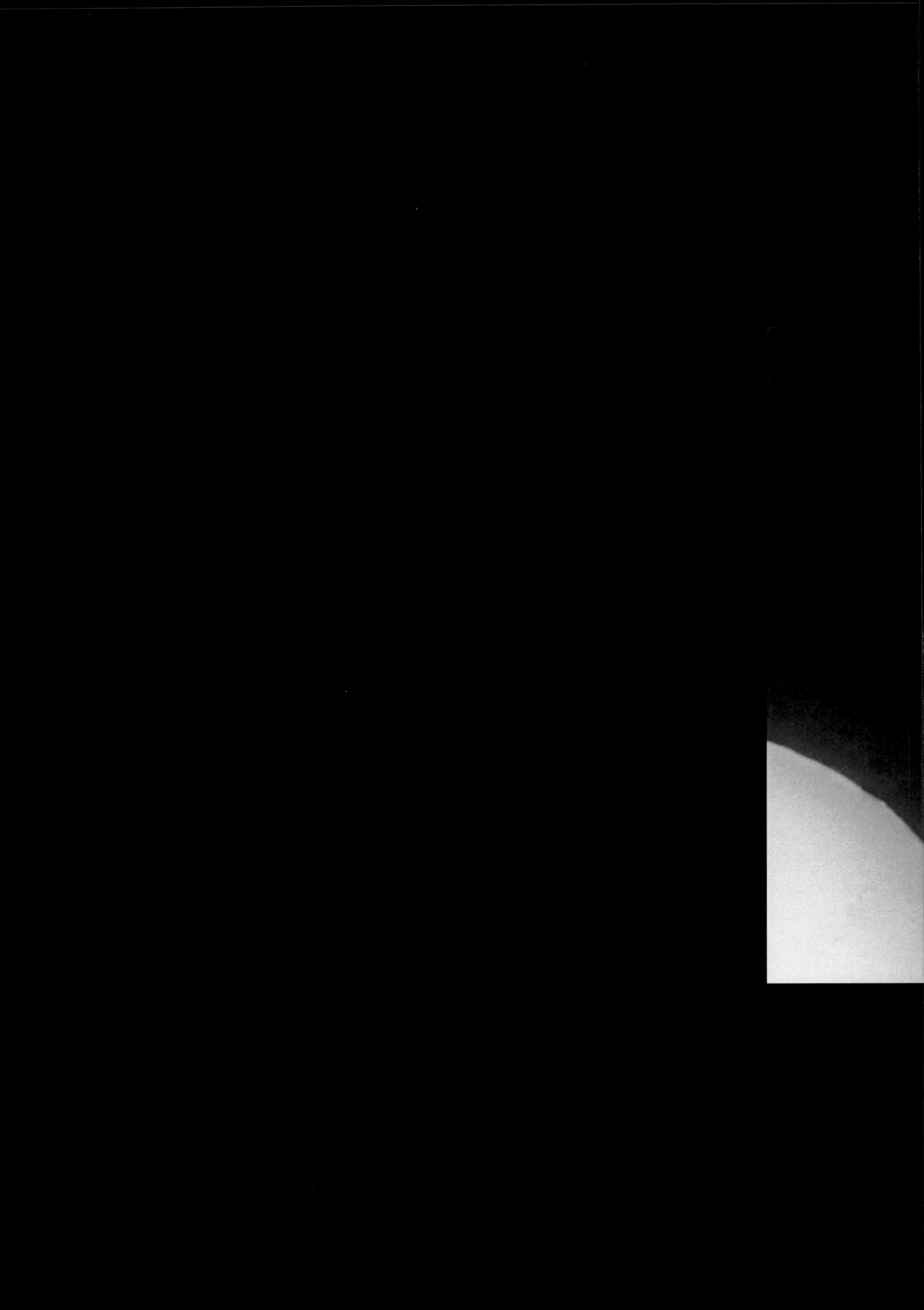

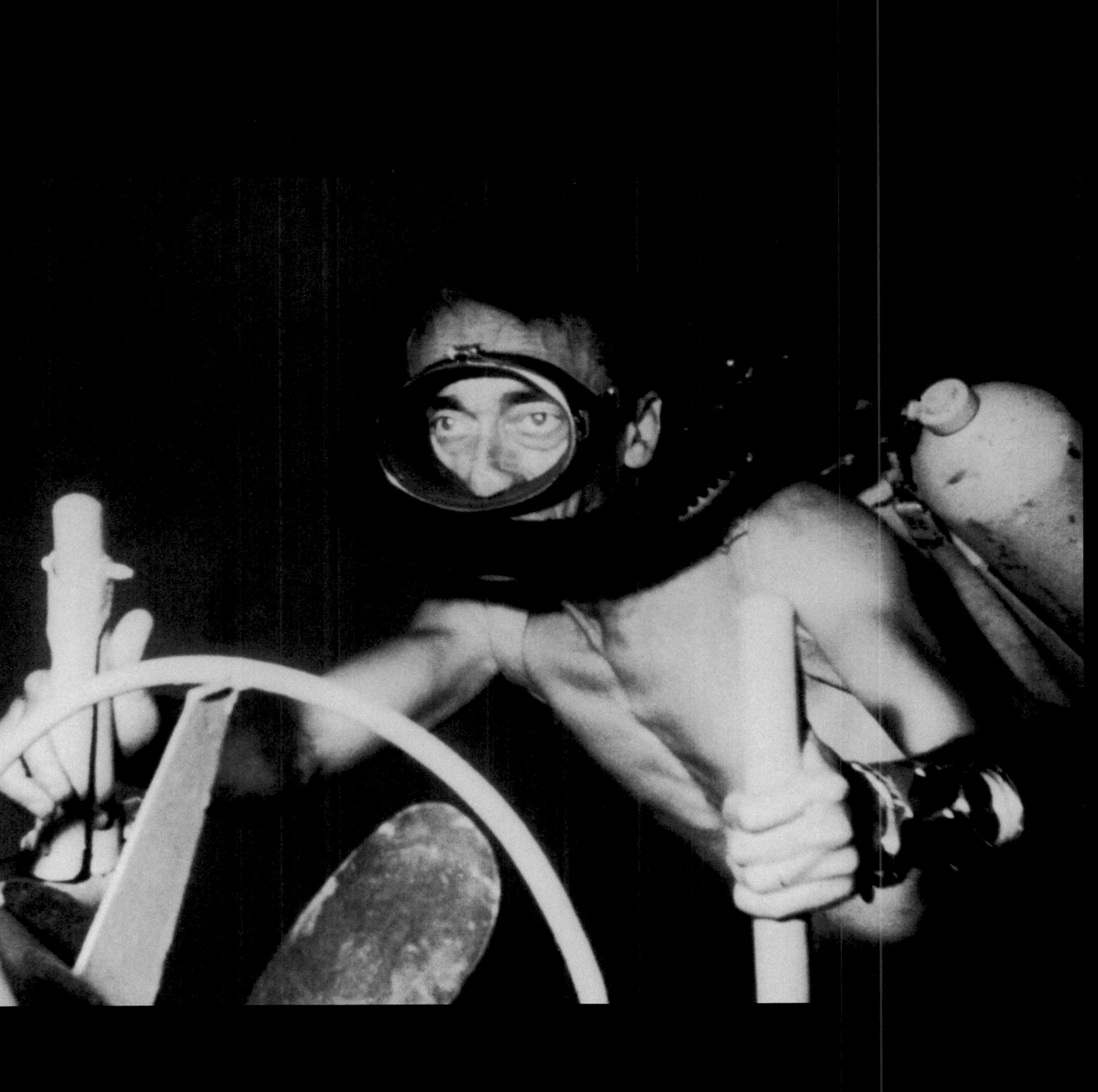

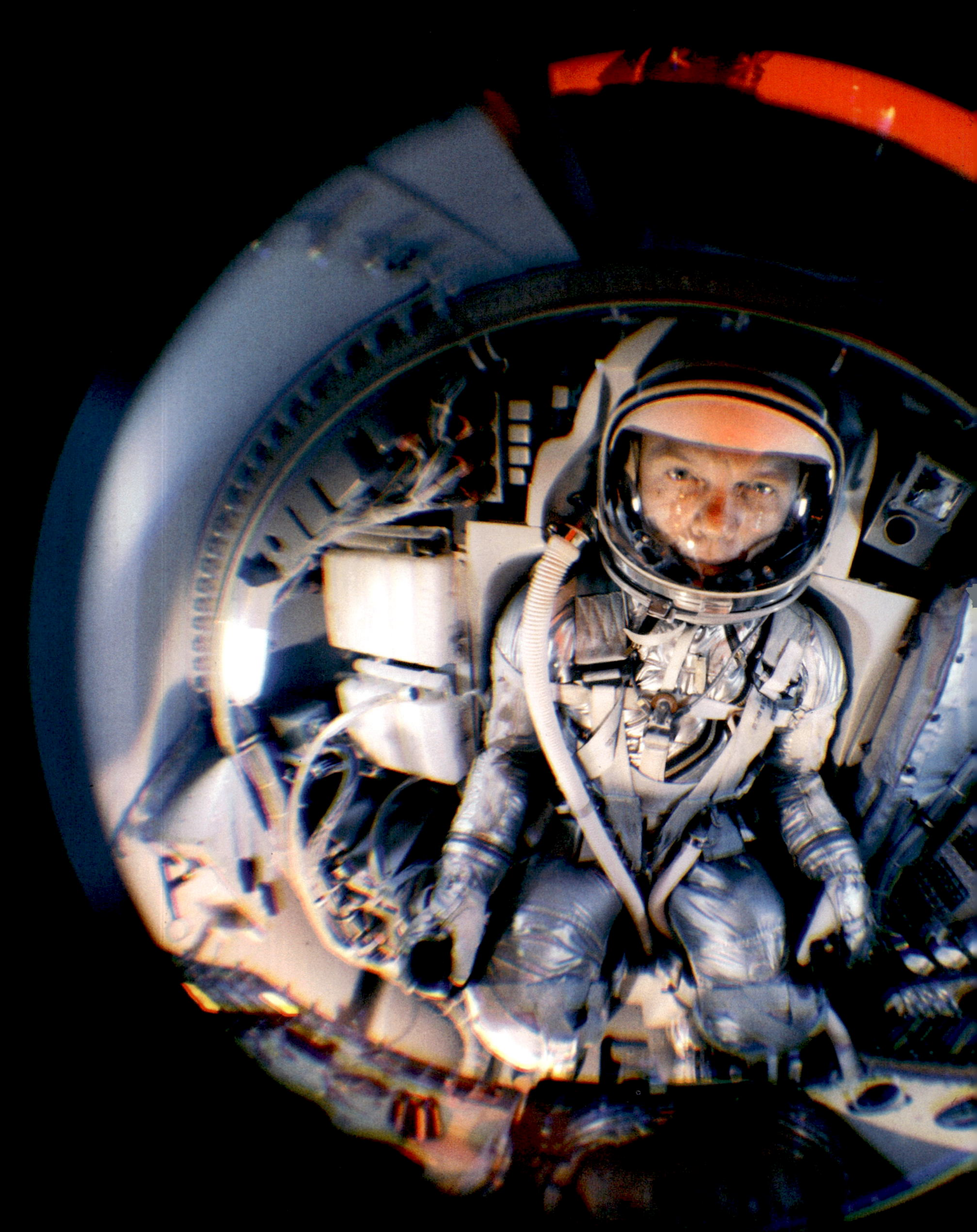

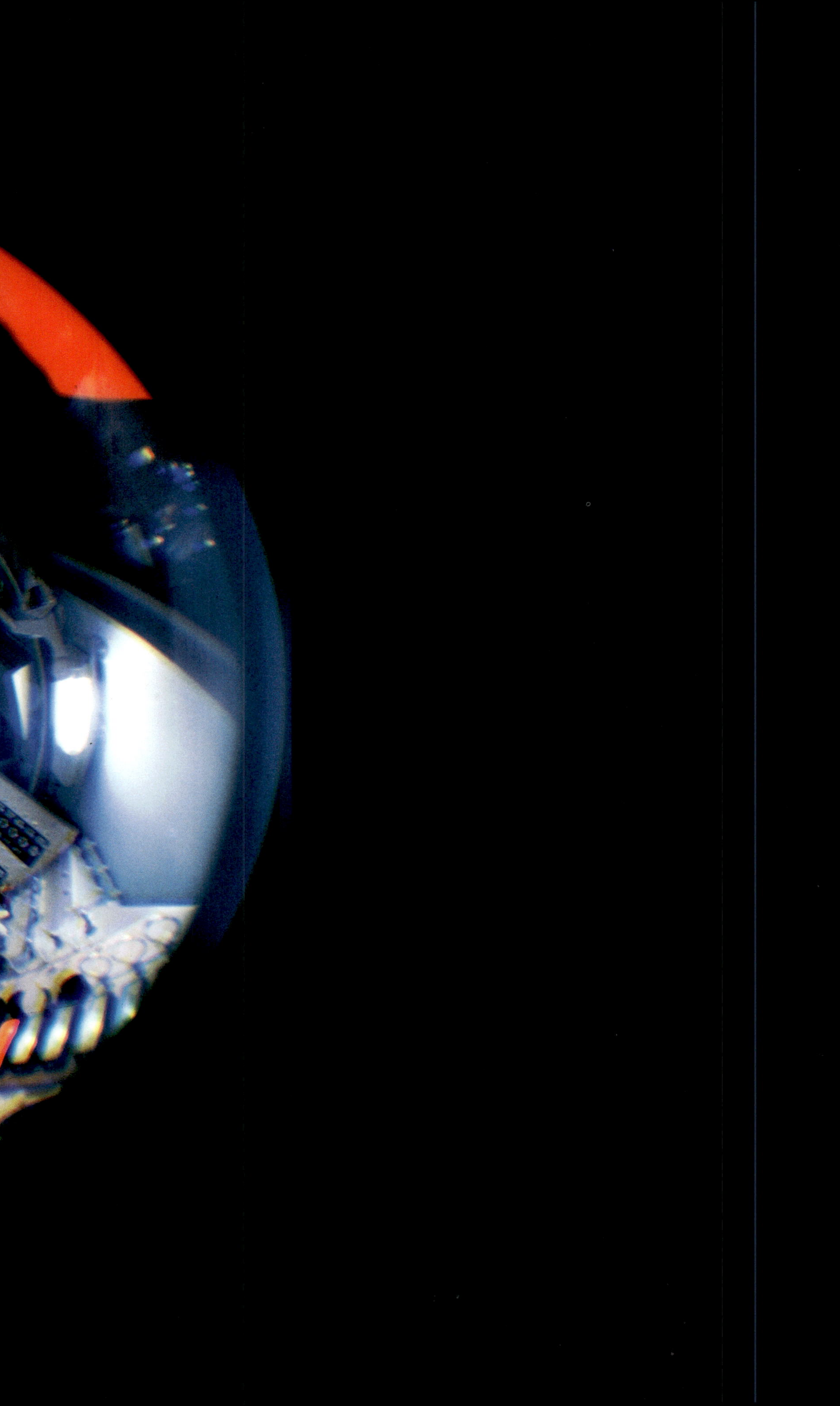

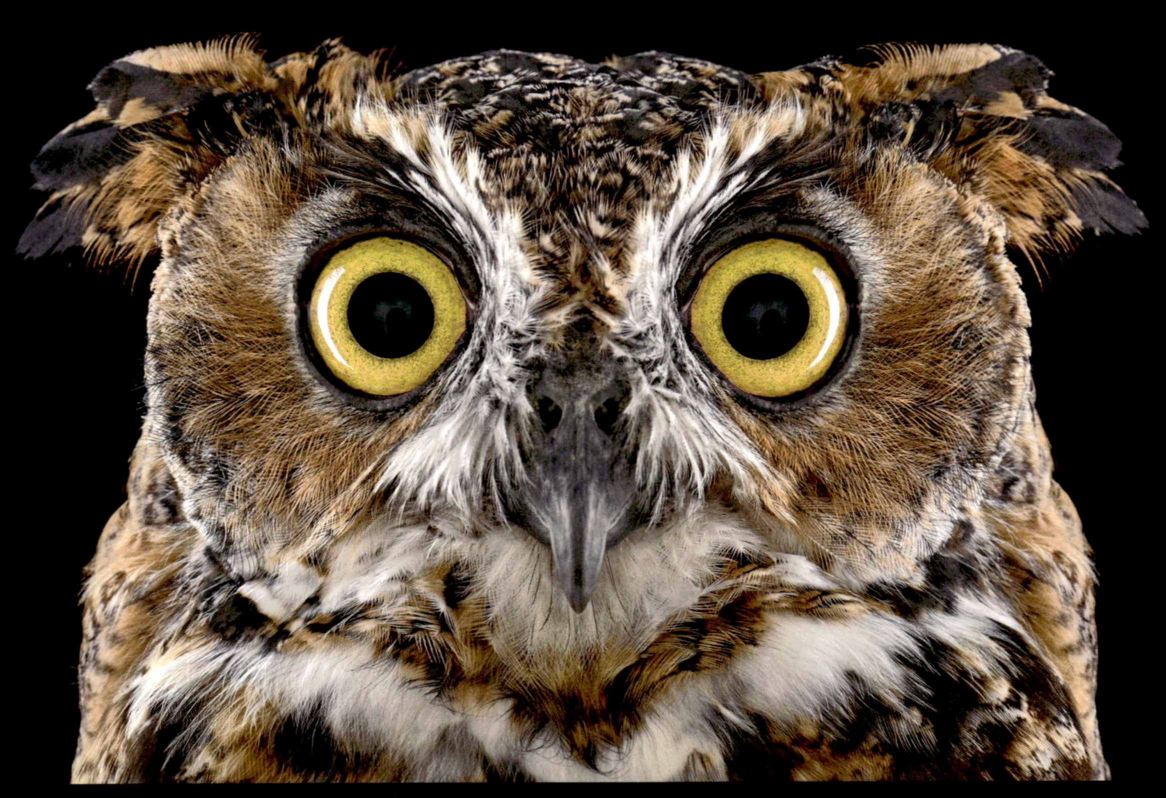

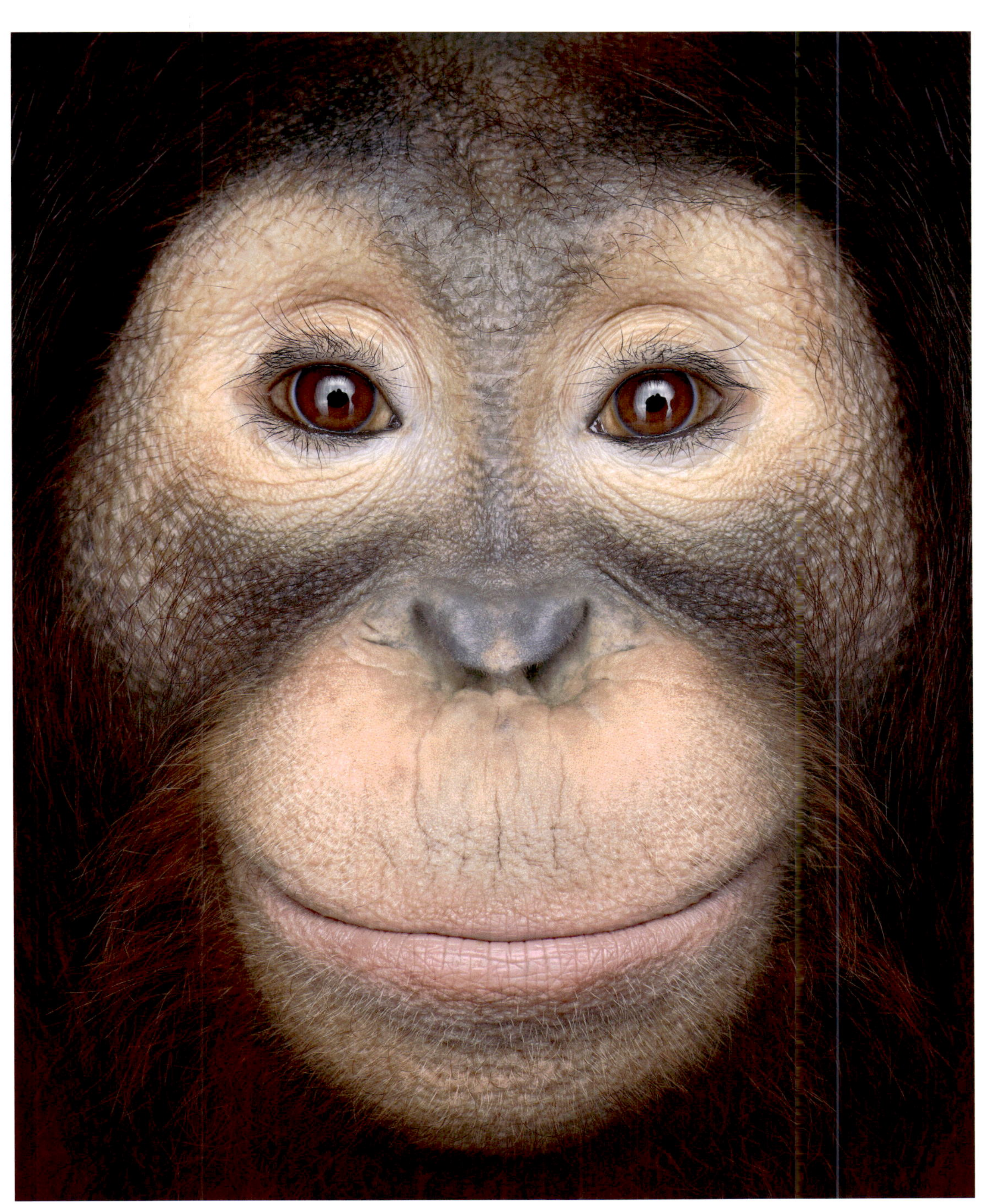

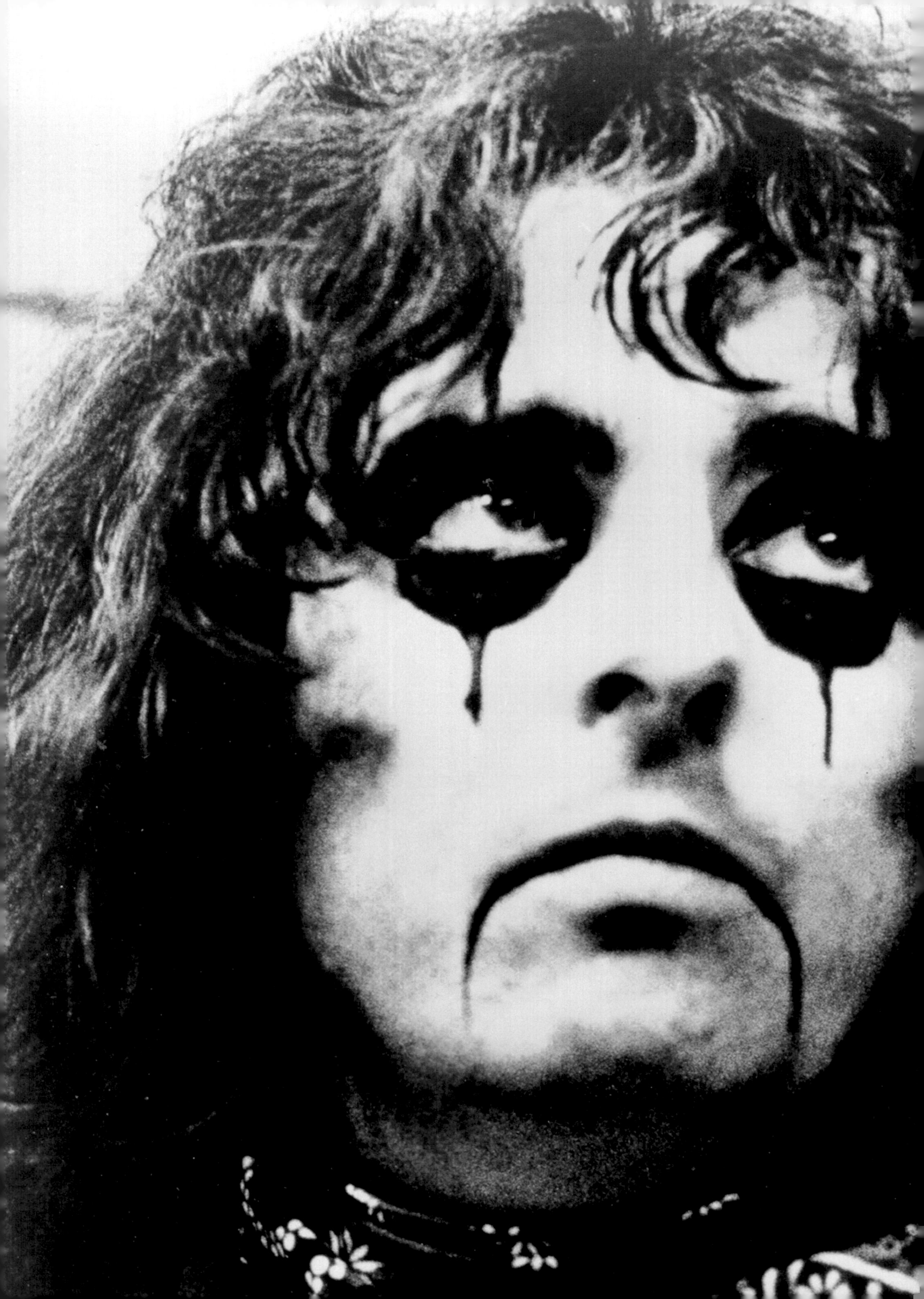

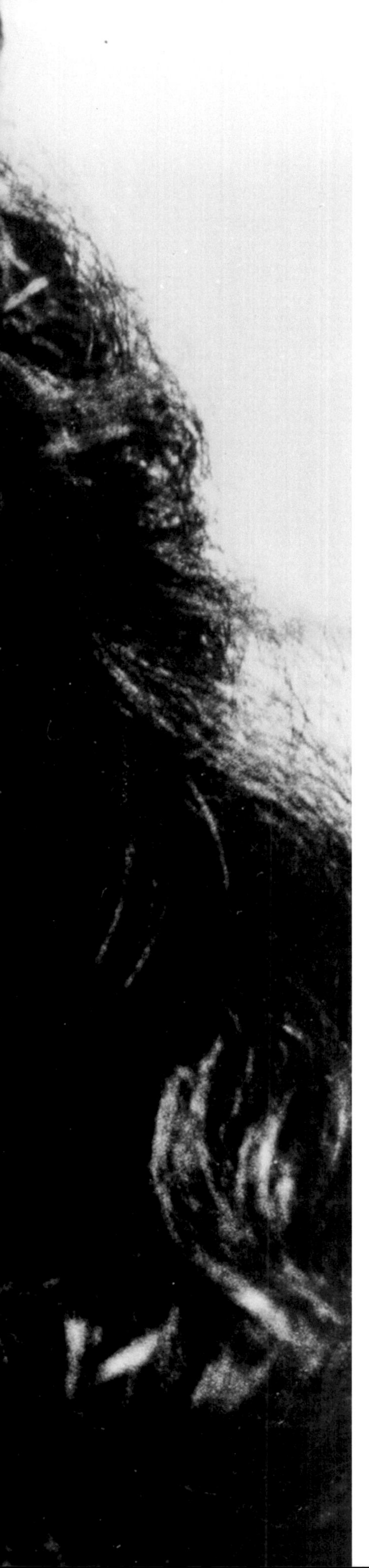

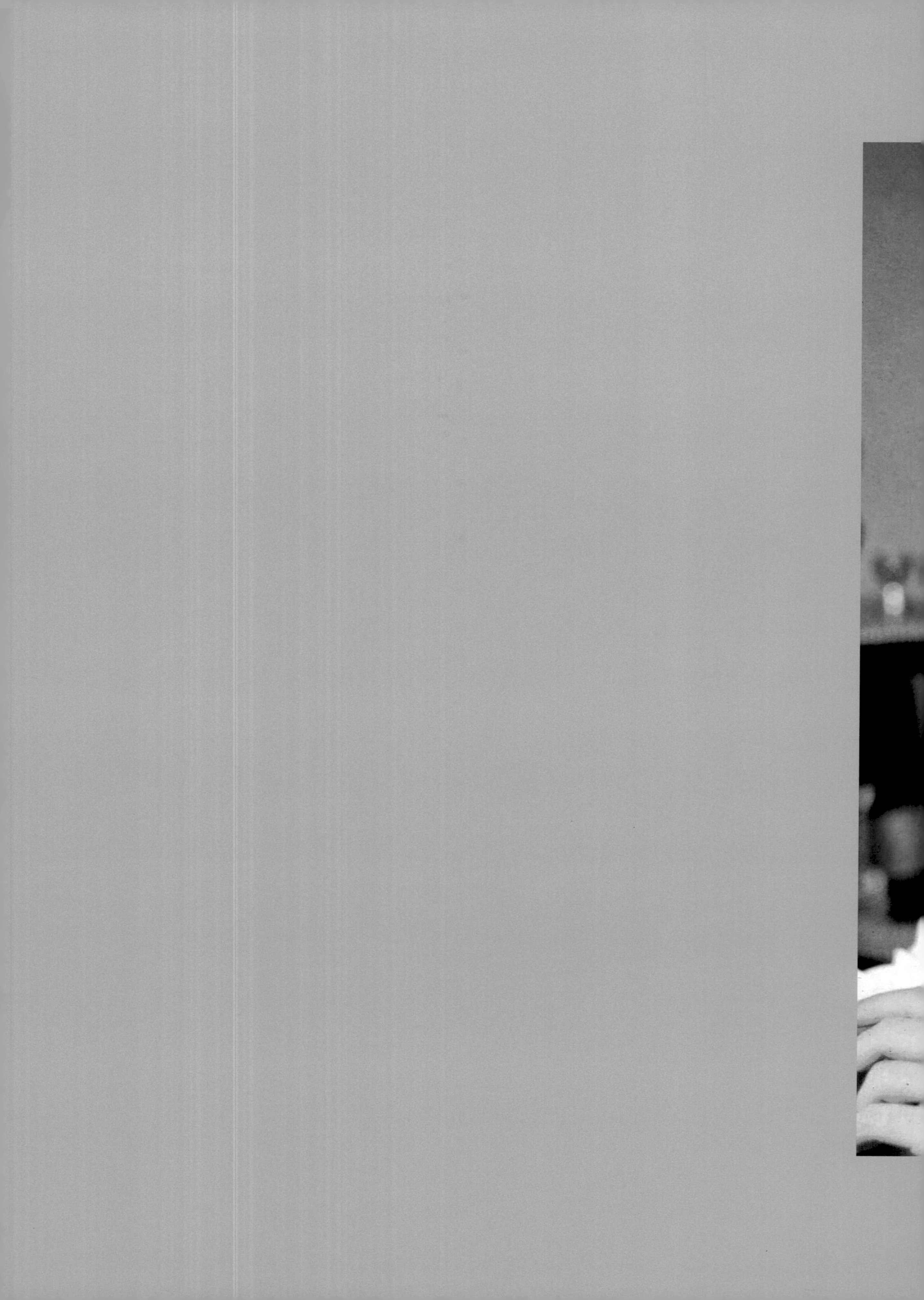

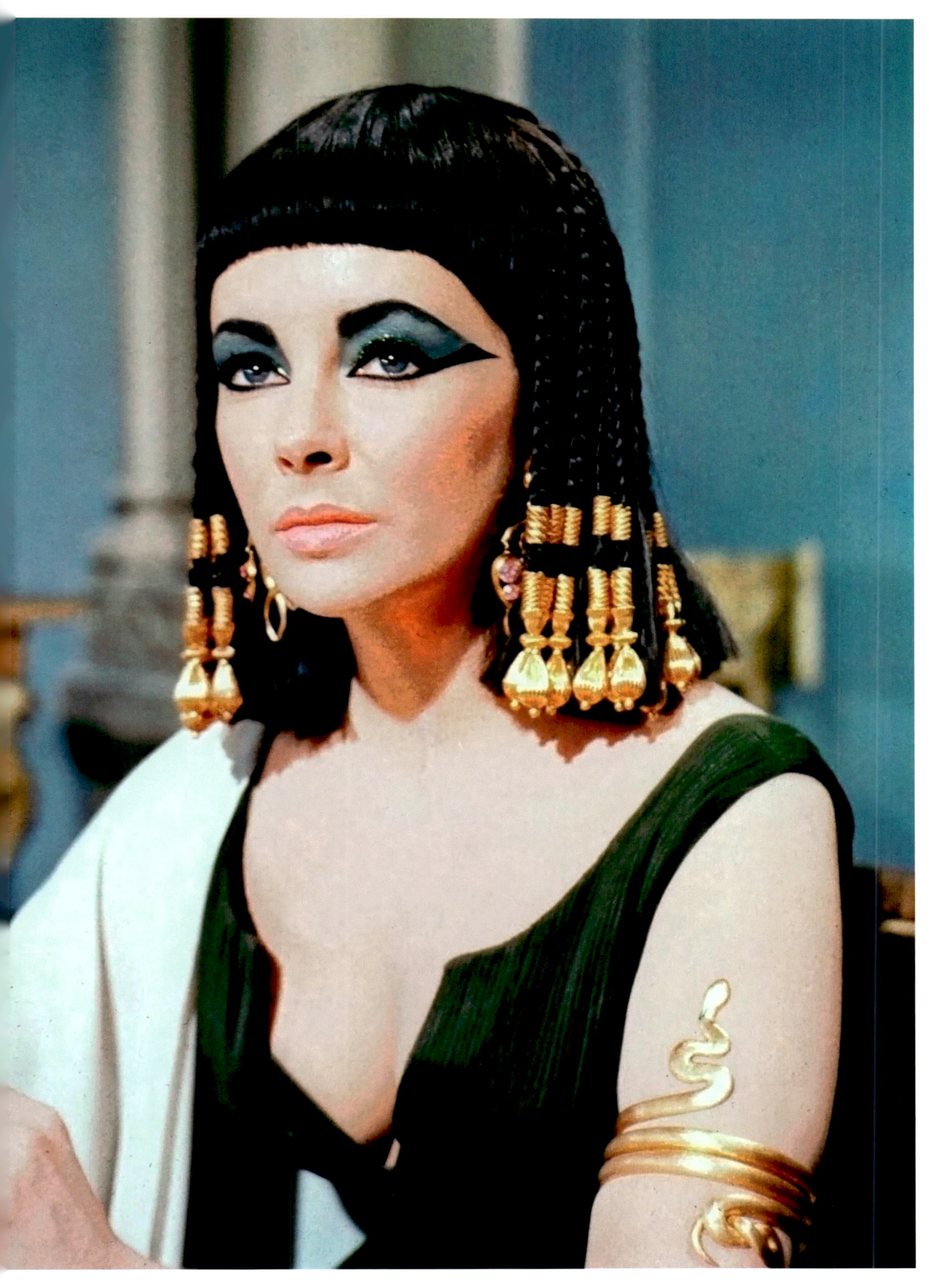

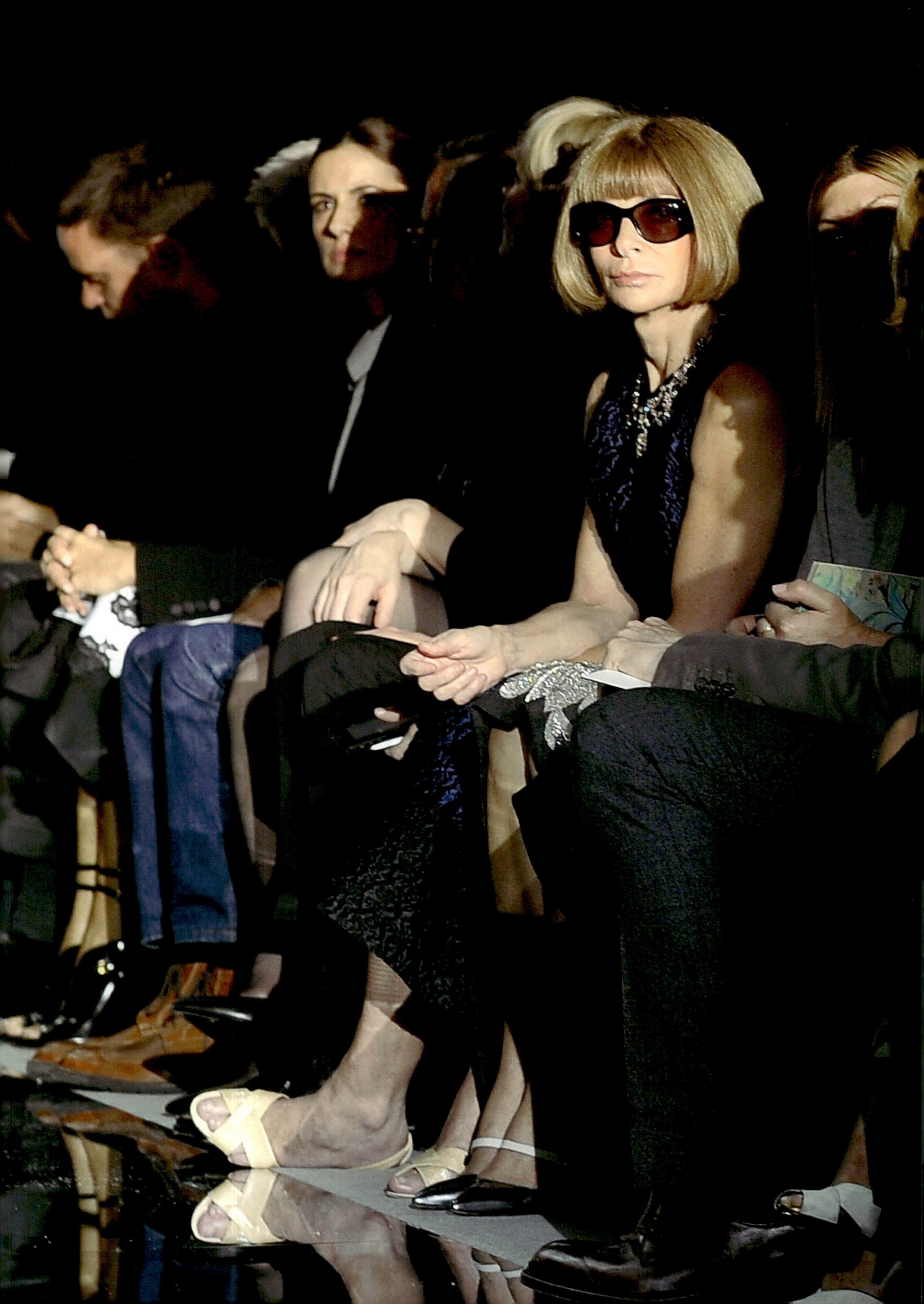

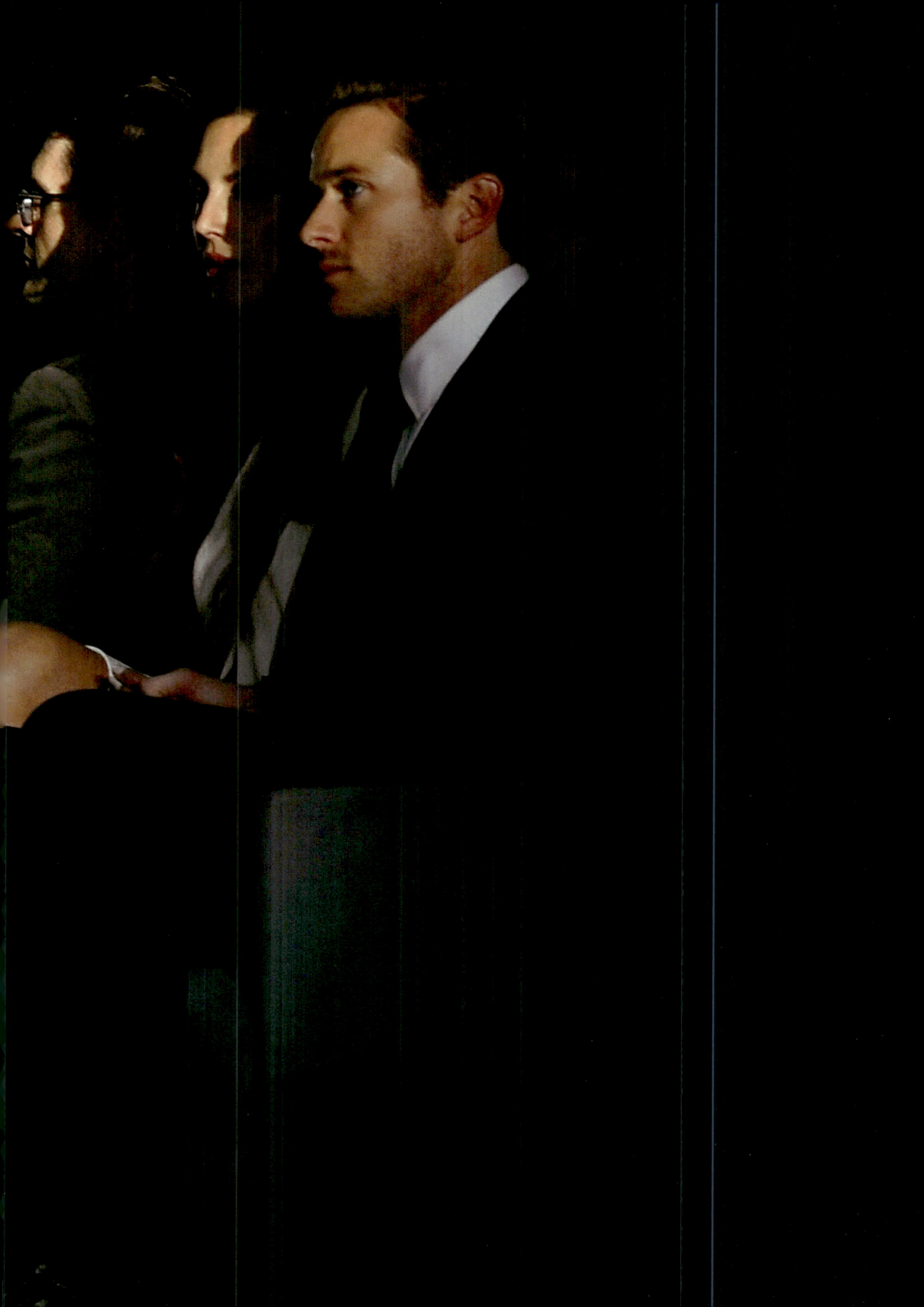

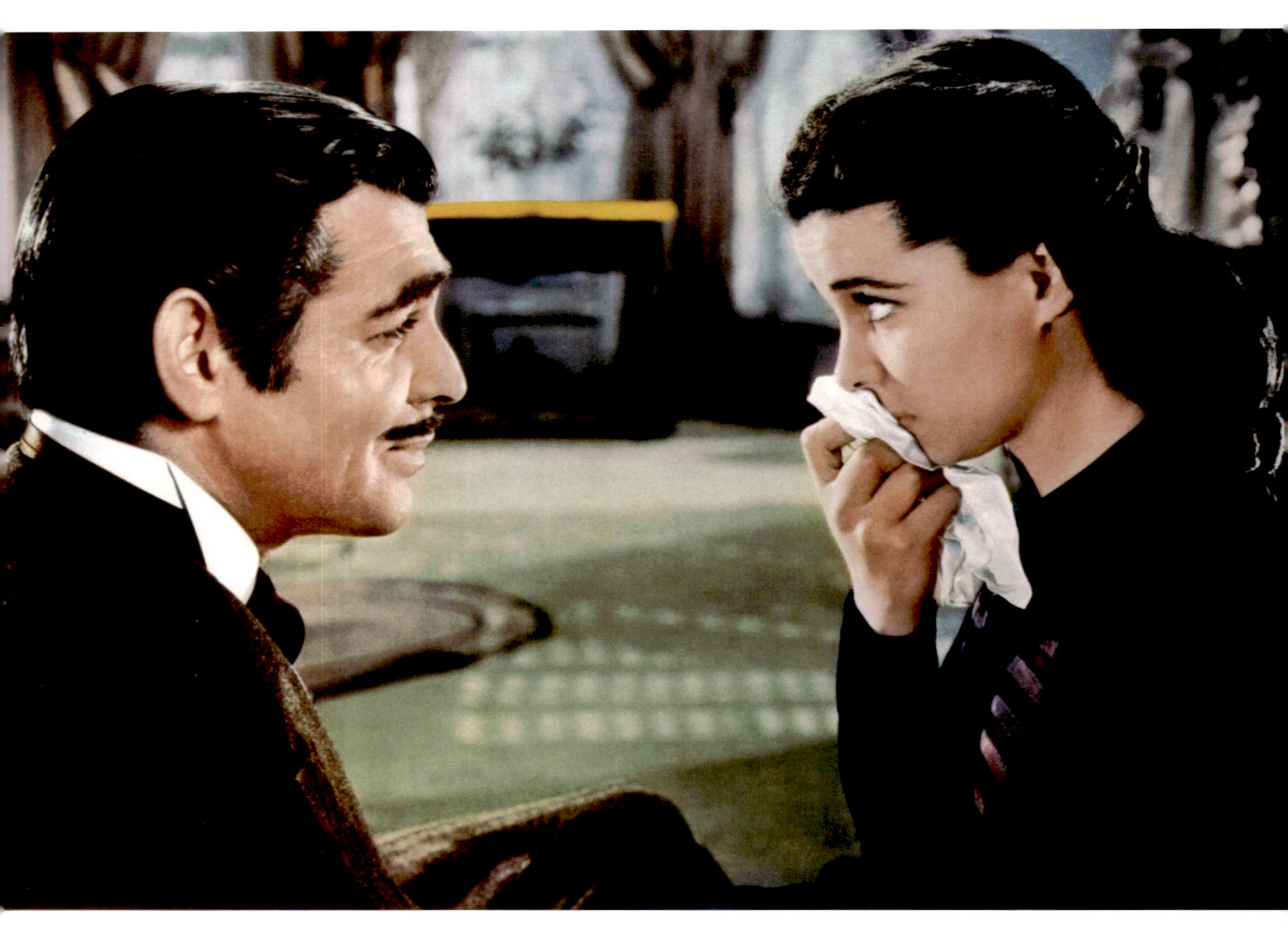

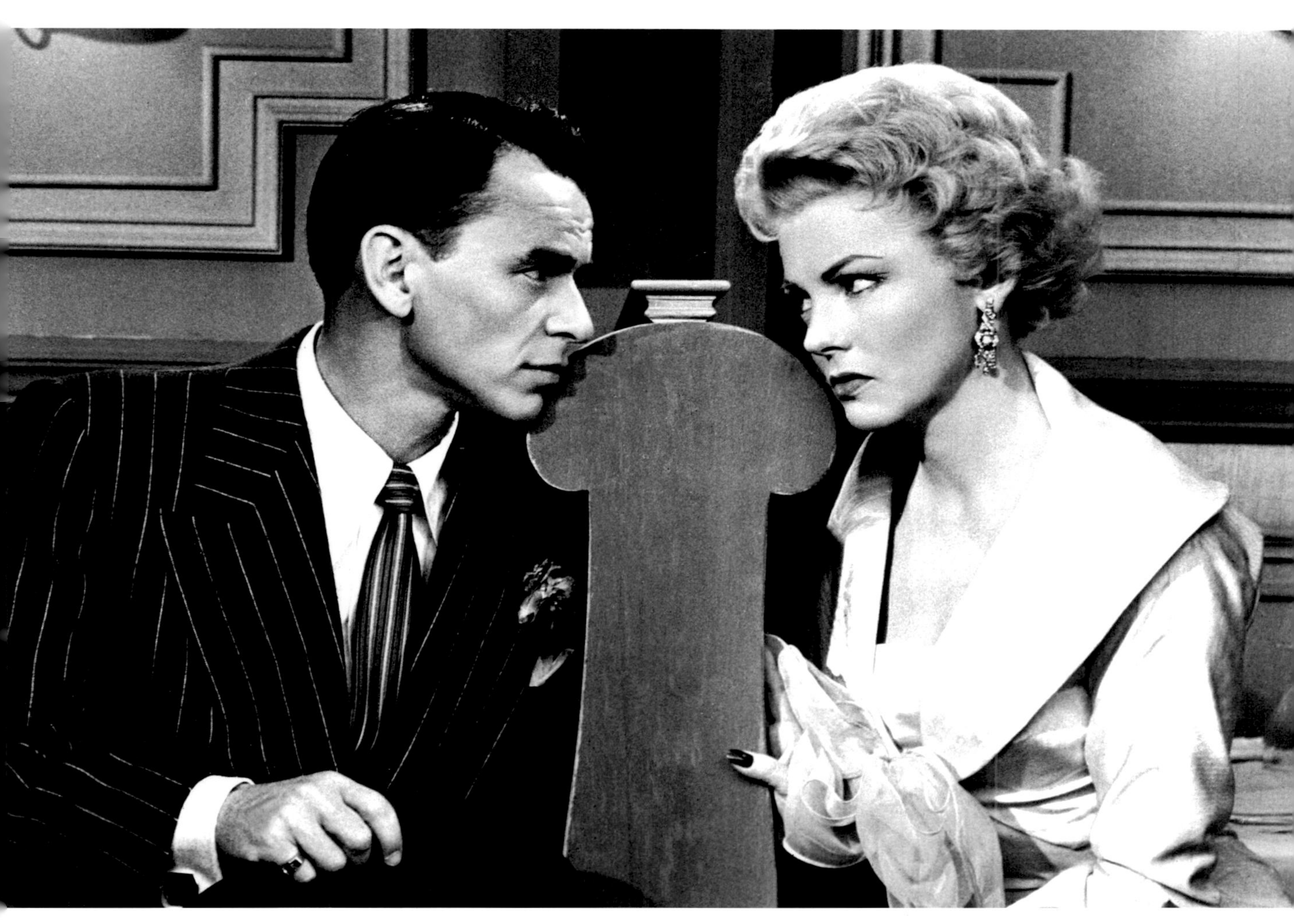

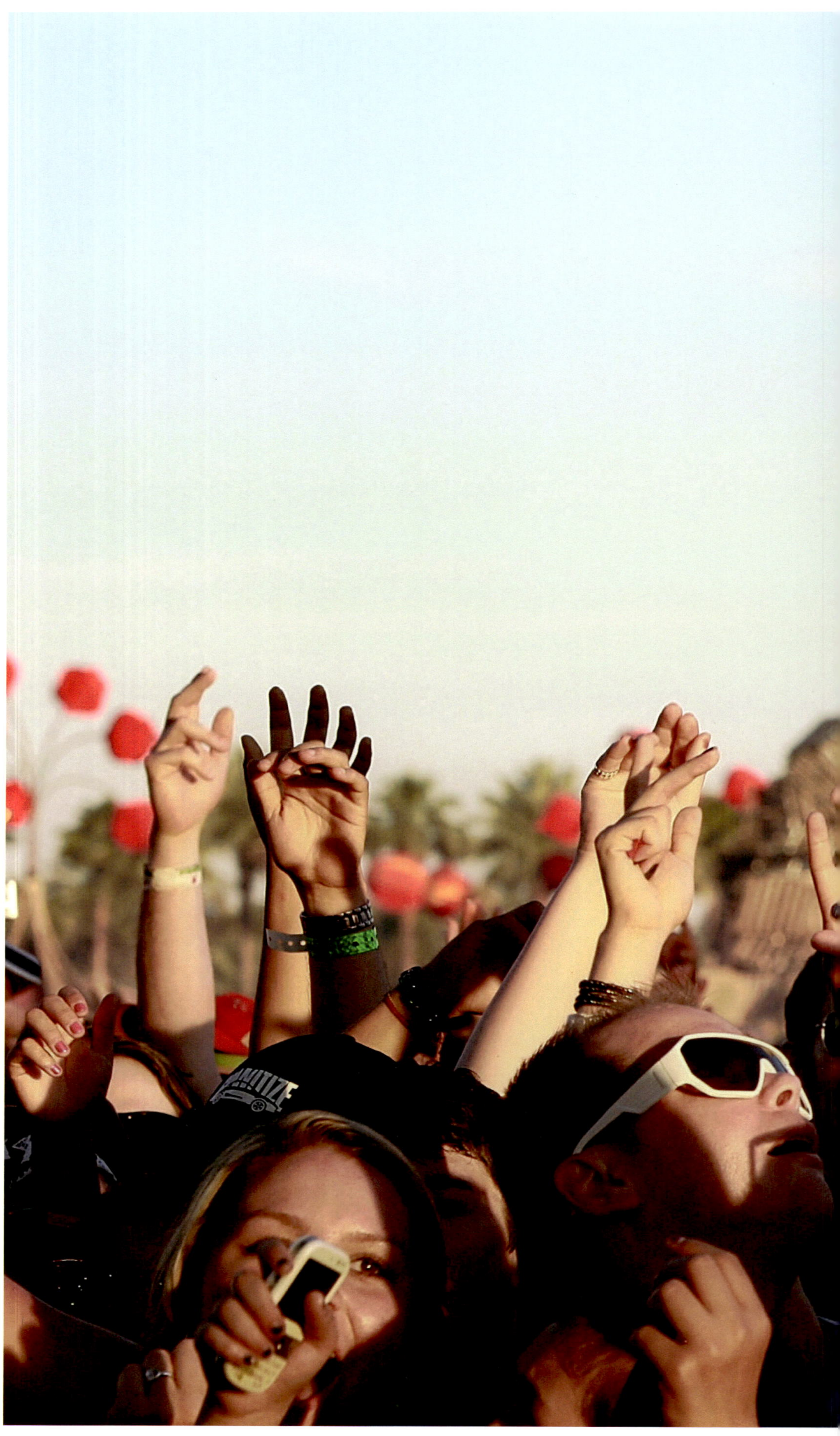

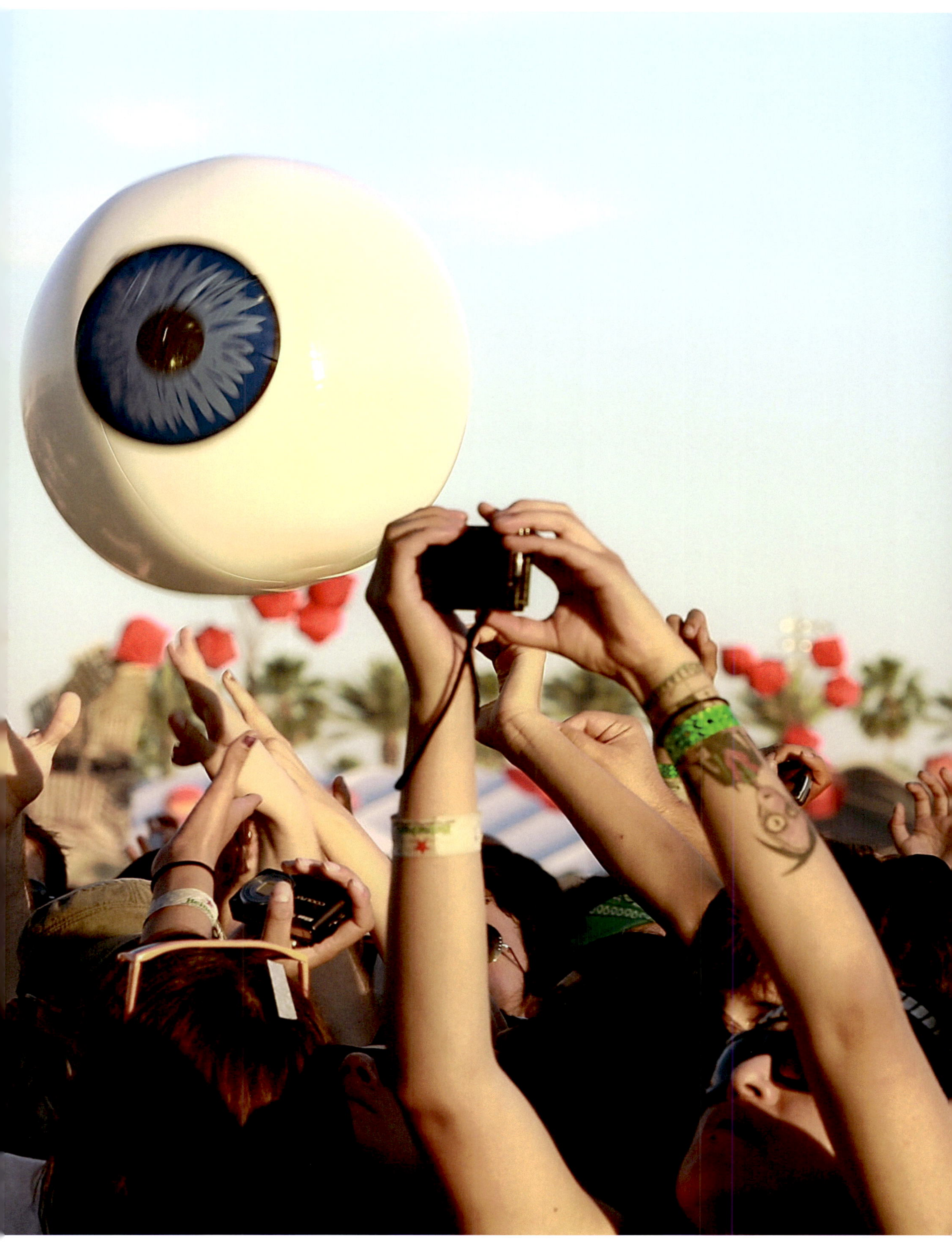

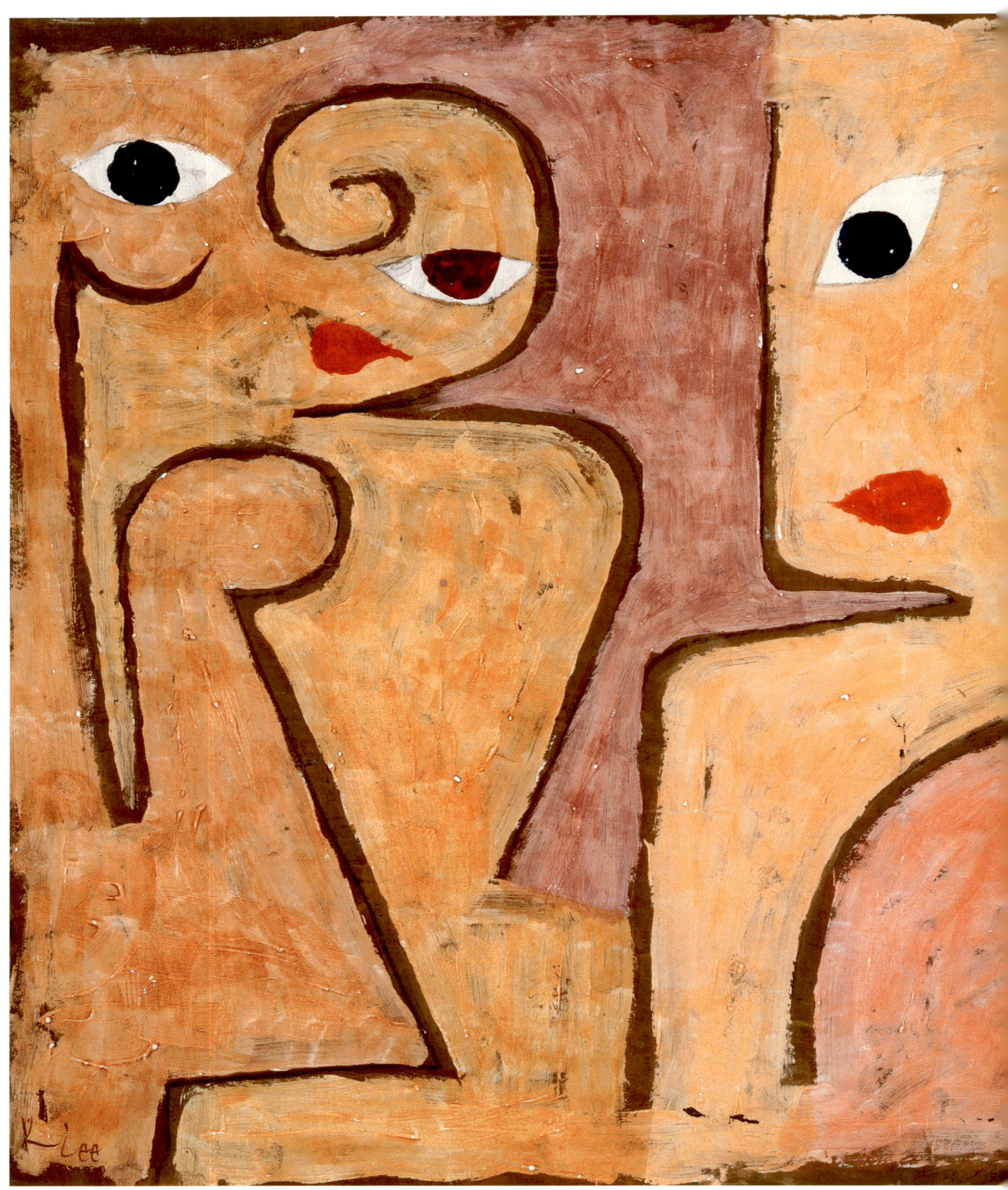

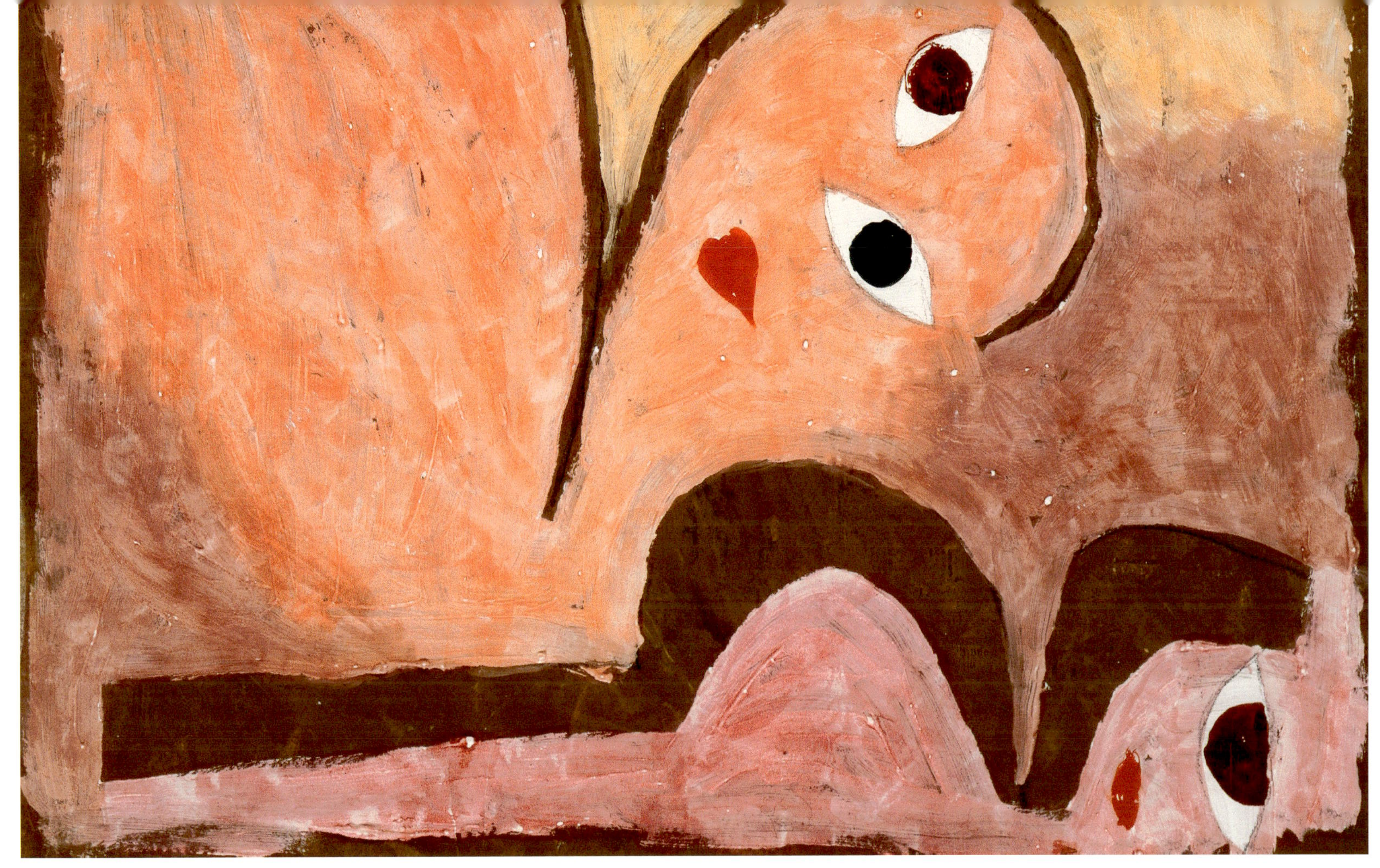

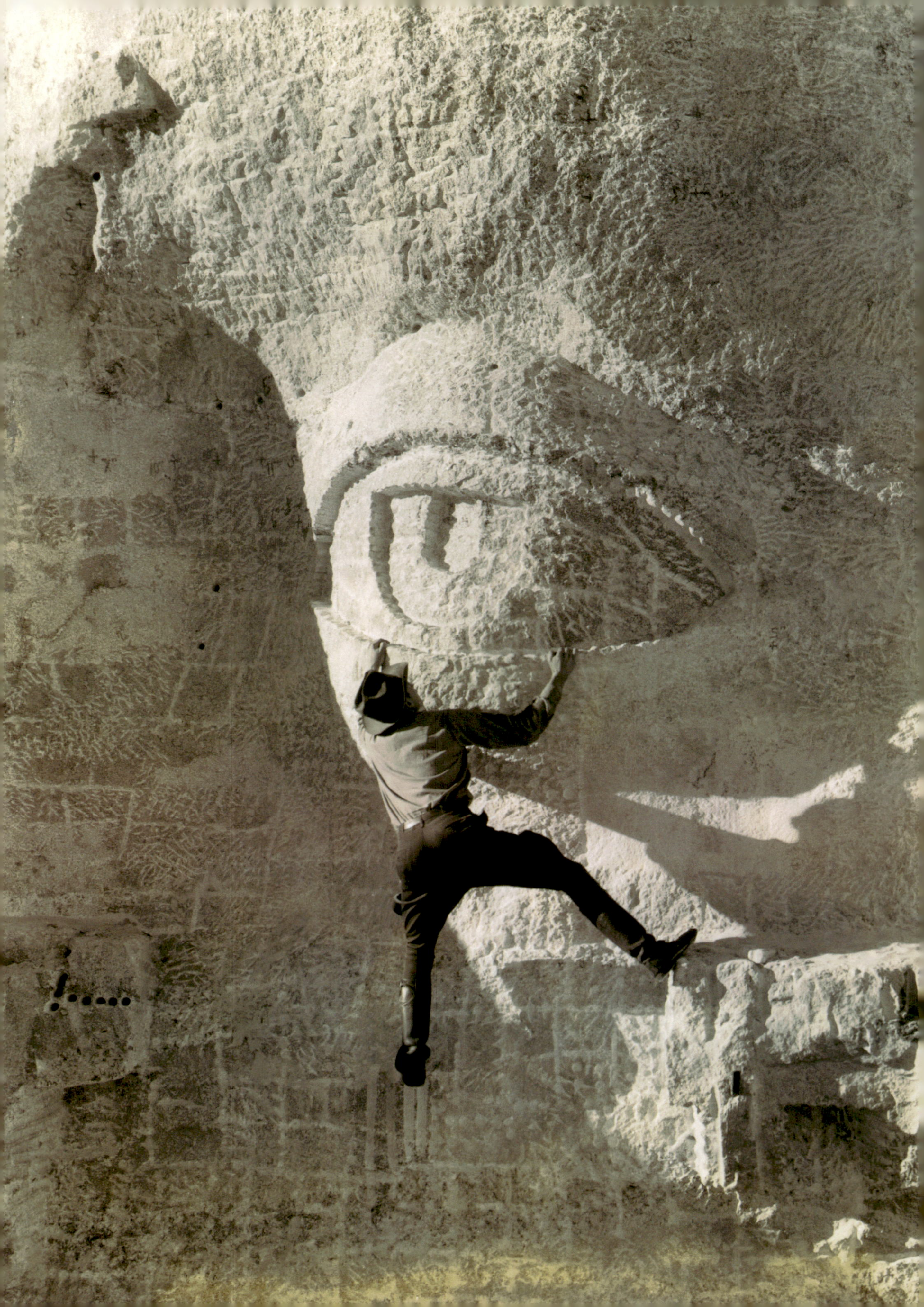

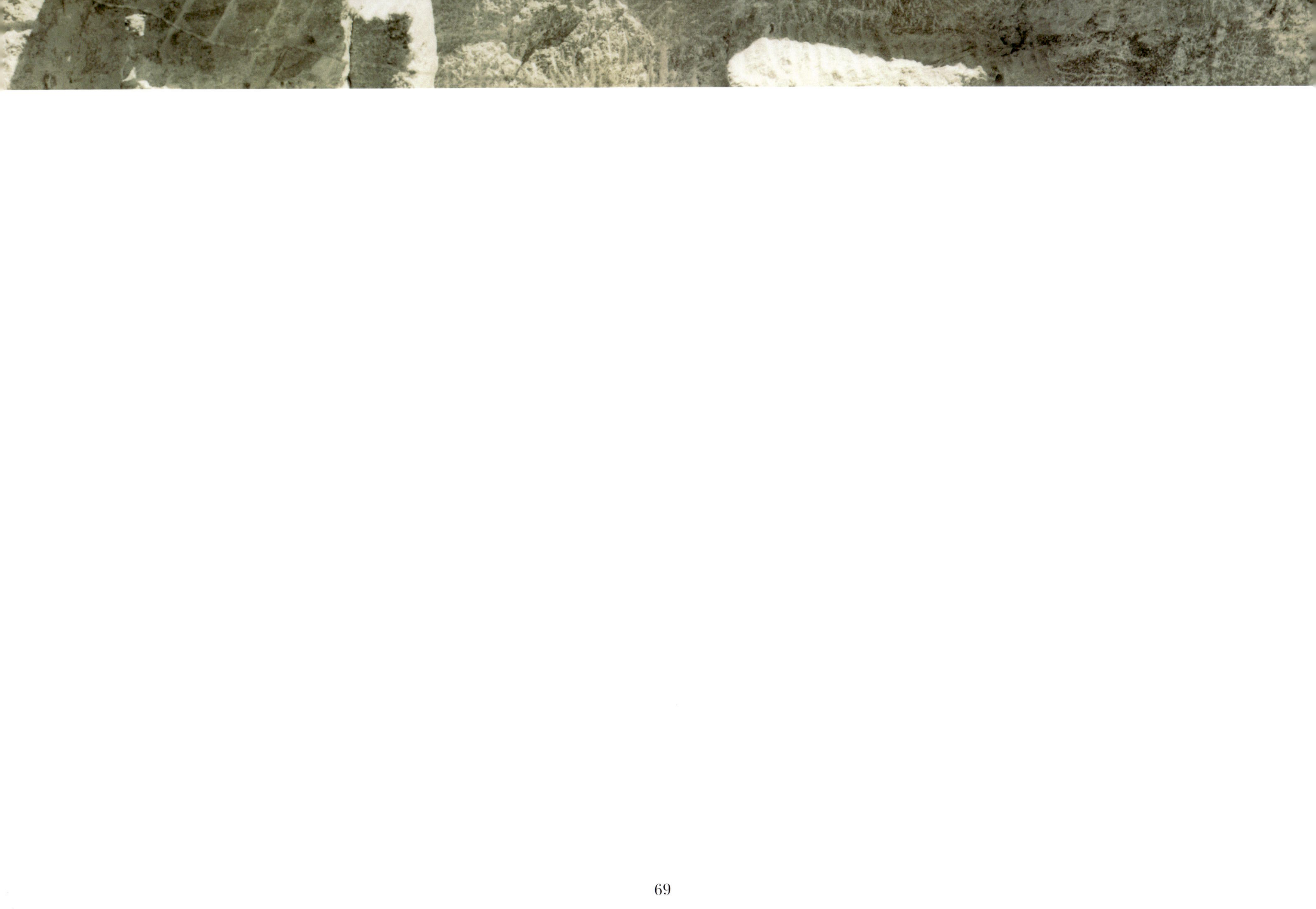

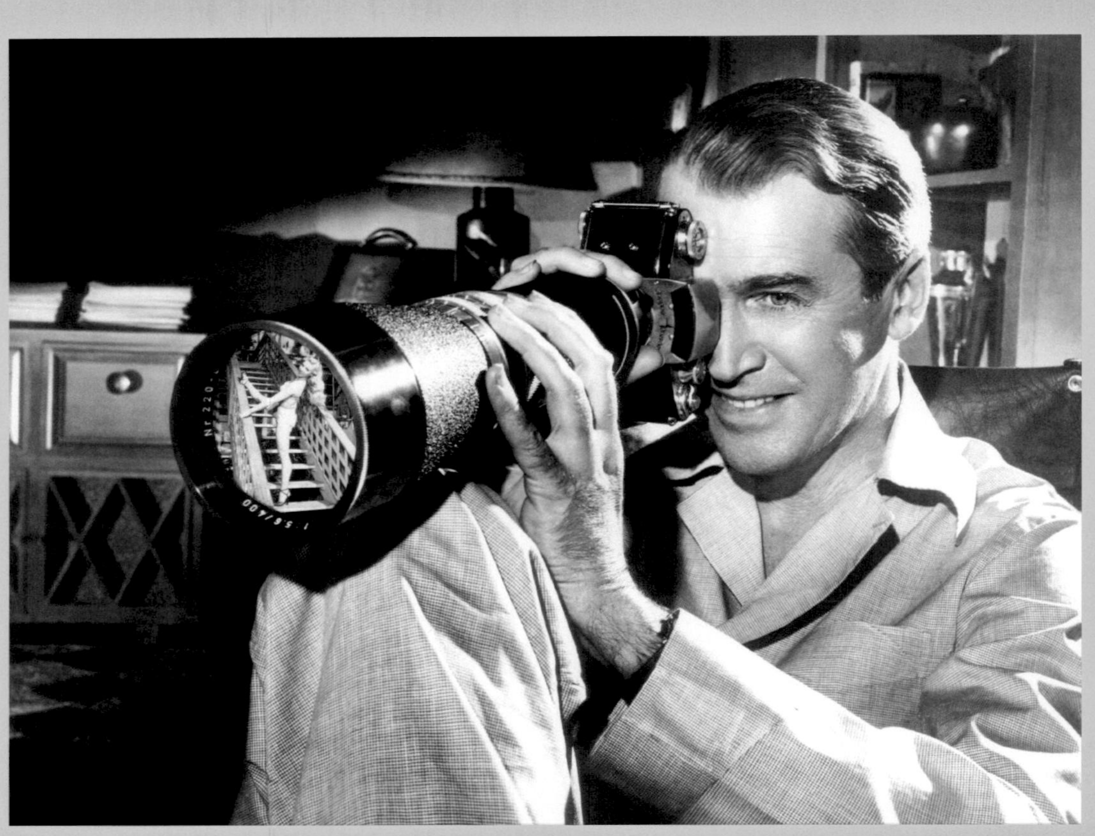

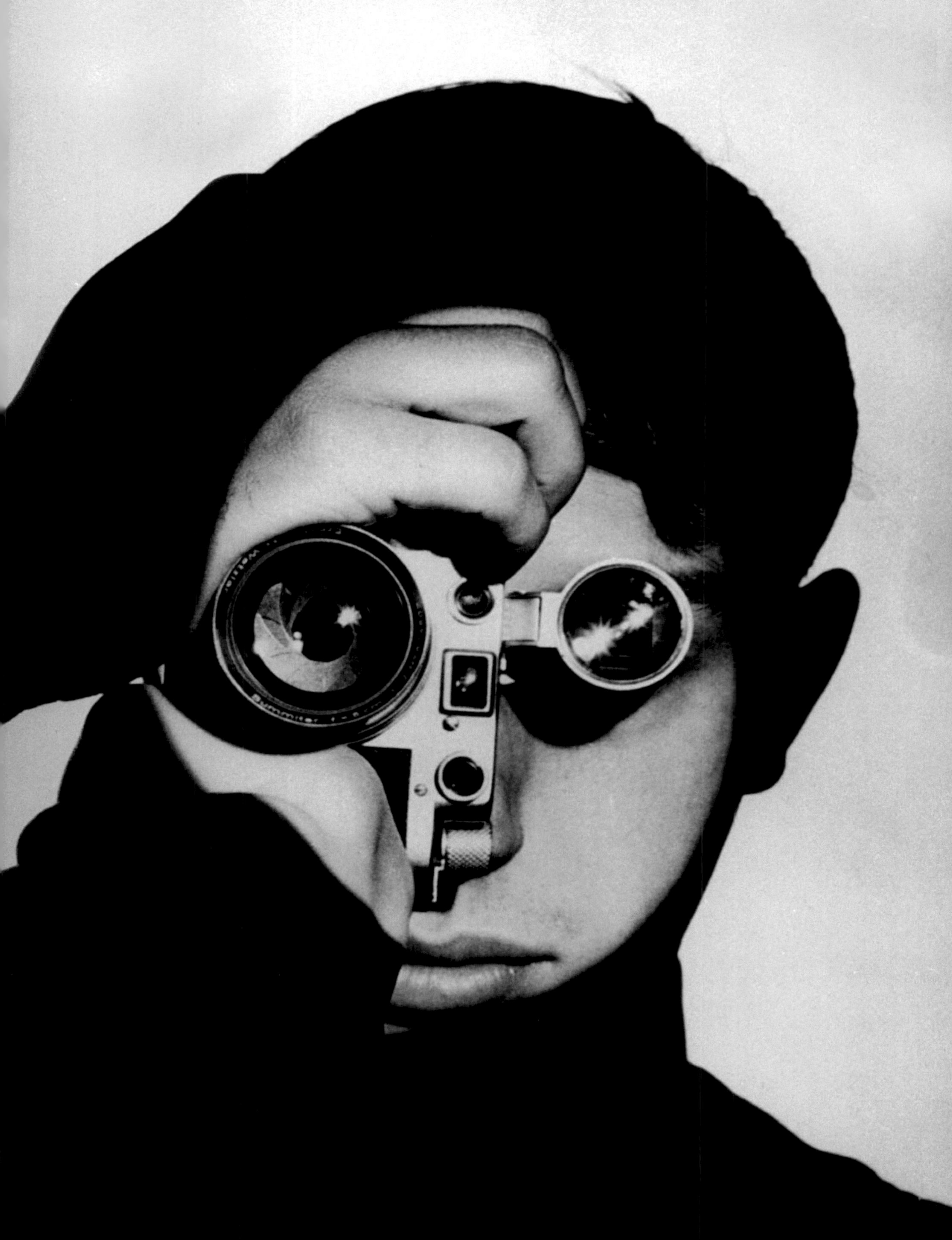

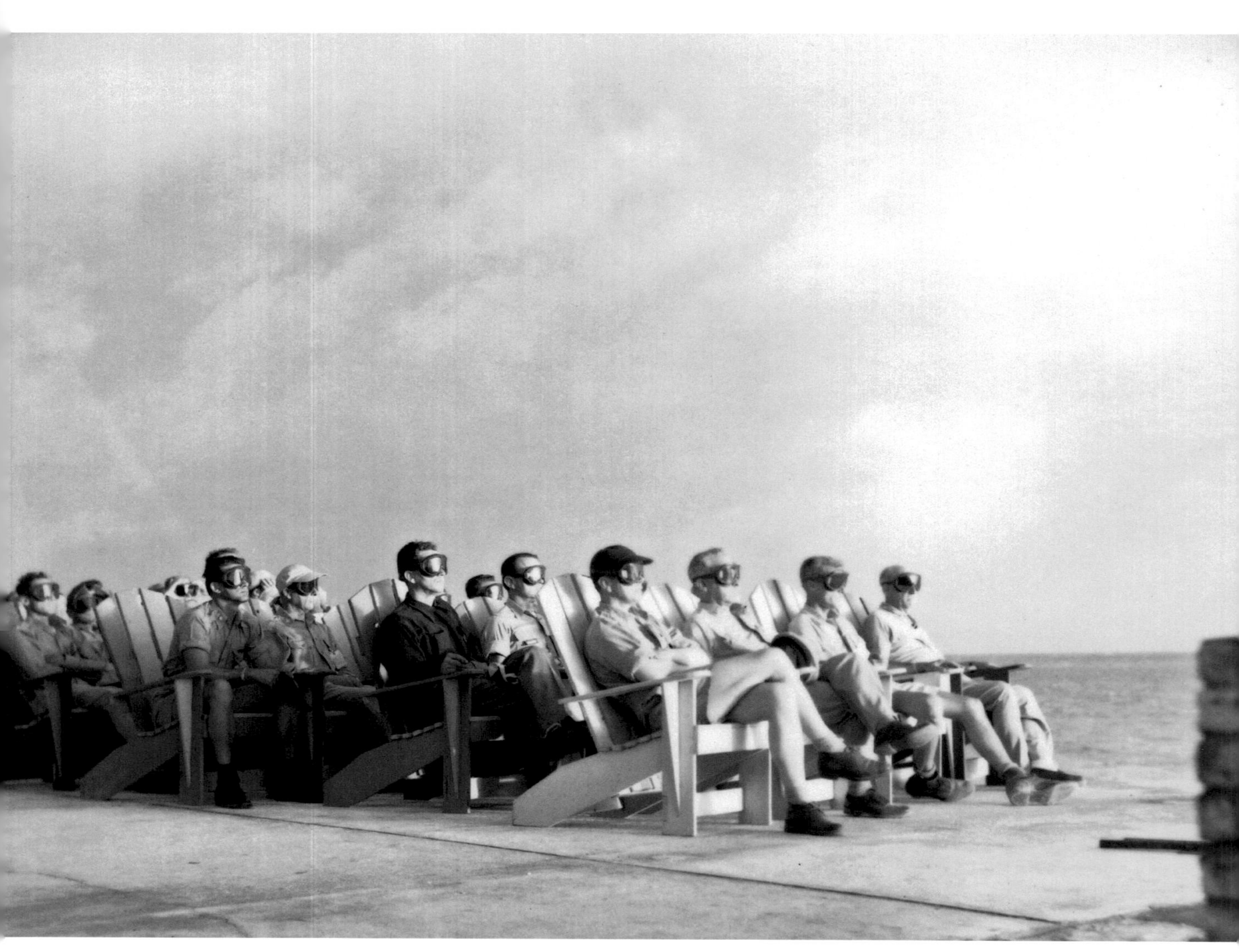

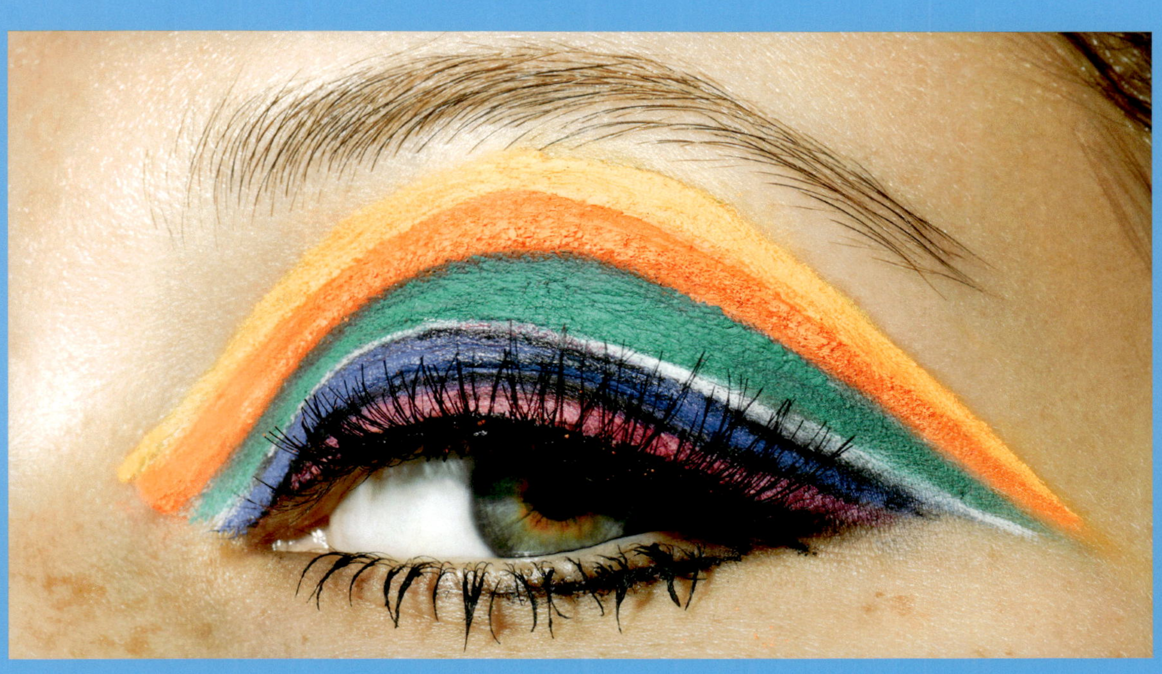

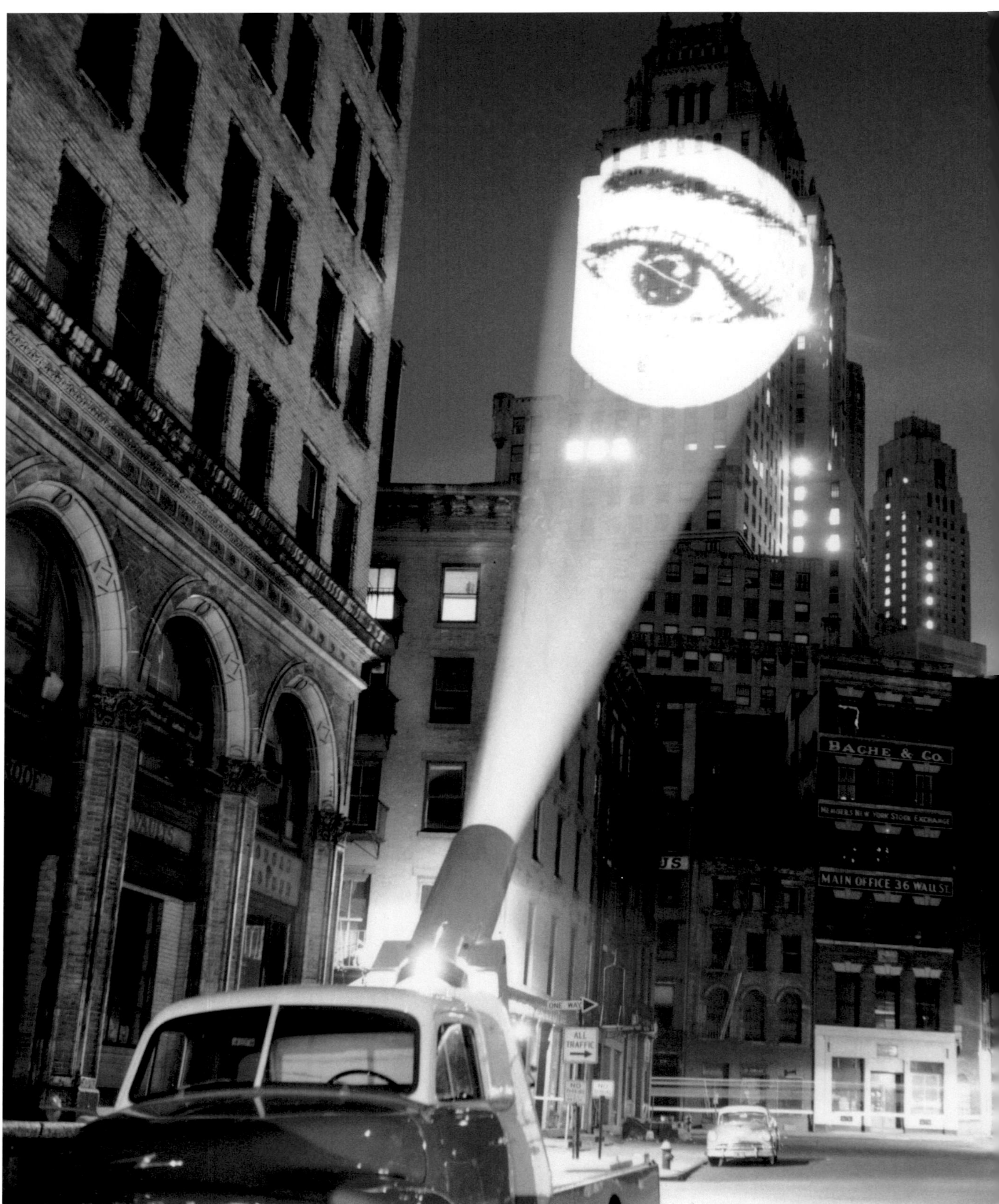
BACHE & CO.
MEMBERS NEW YORK STOCK EXCHANGE
MAIN OFFICE 36 WALL ST.
ONE WAY
ALL TRAFFIC

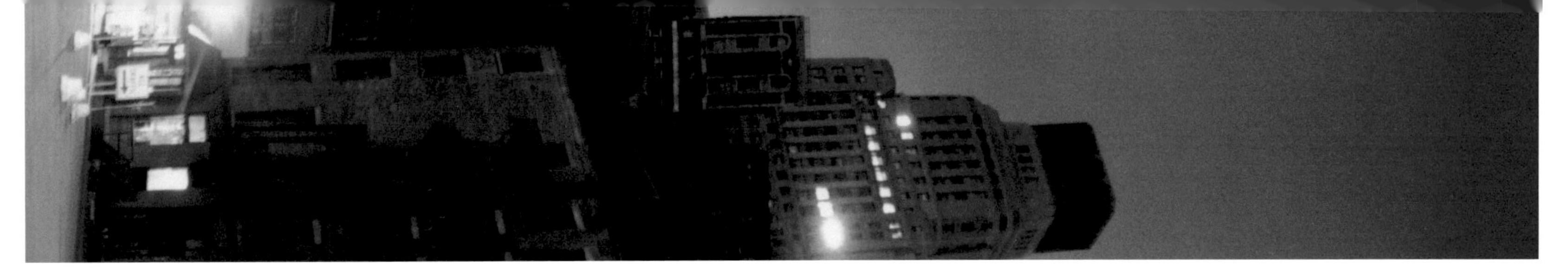

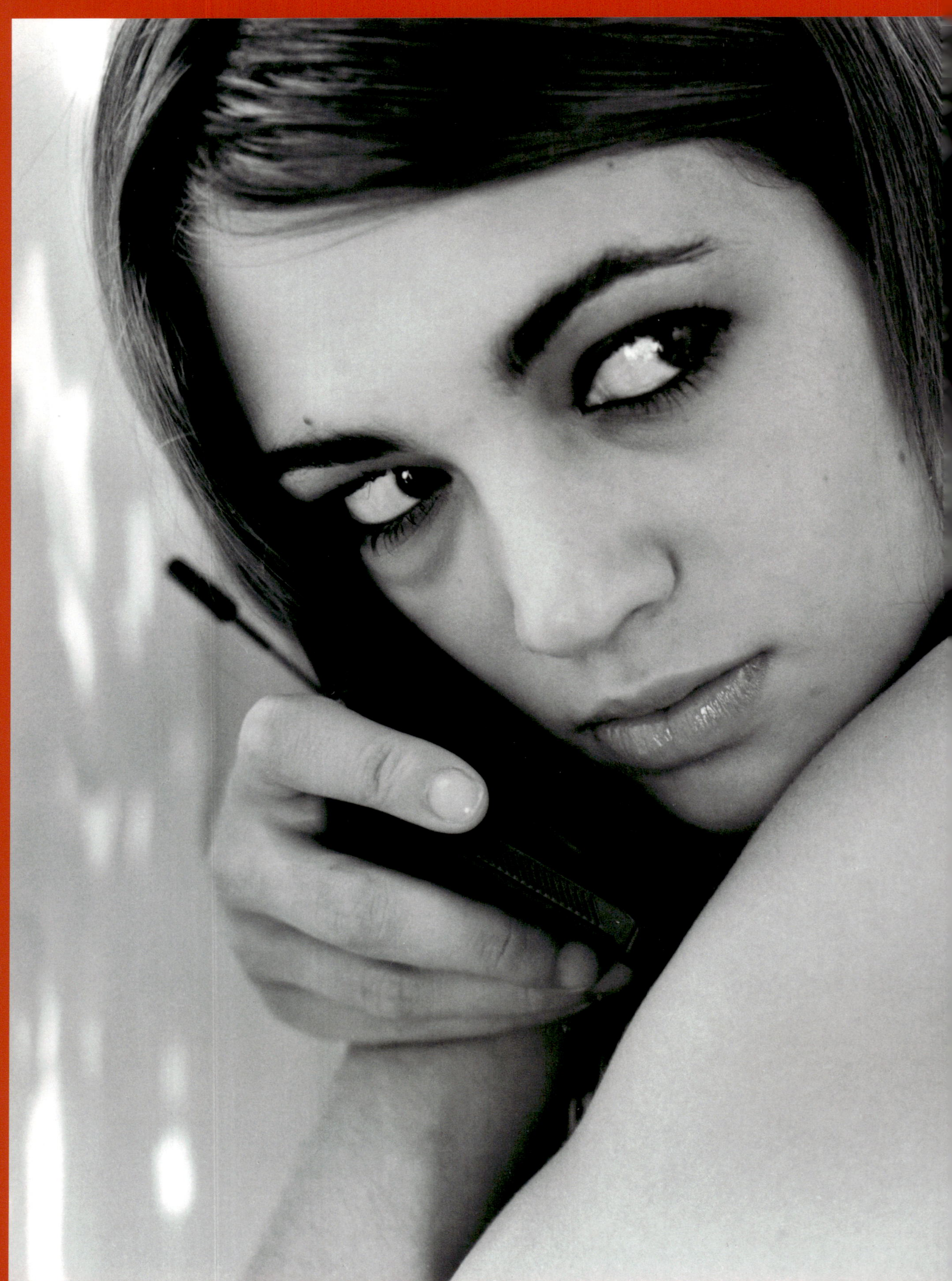

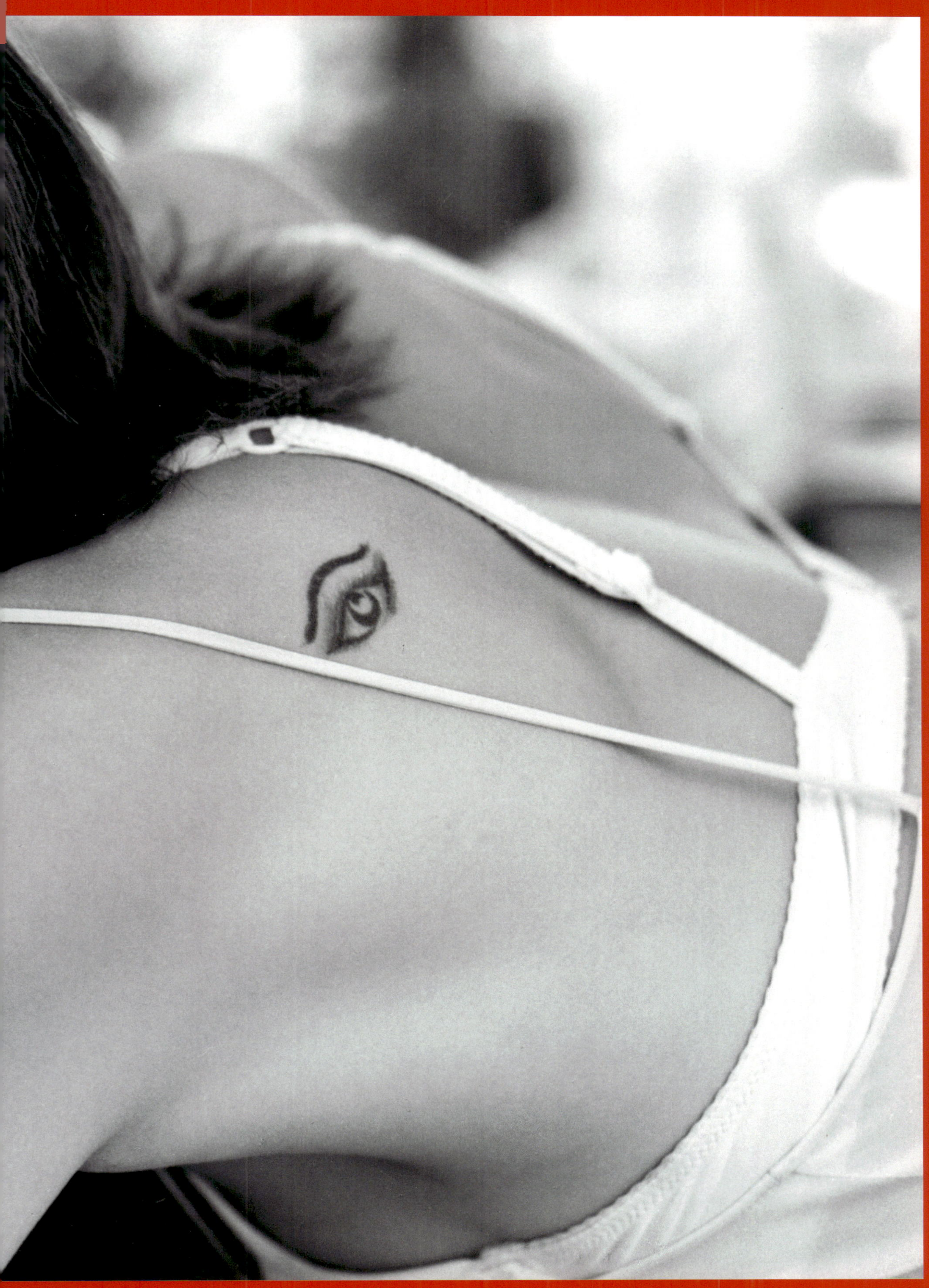

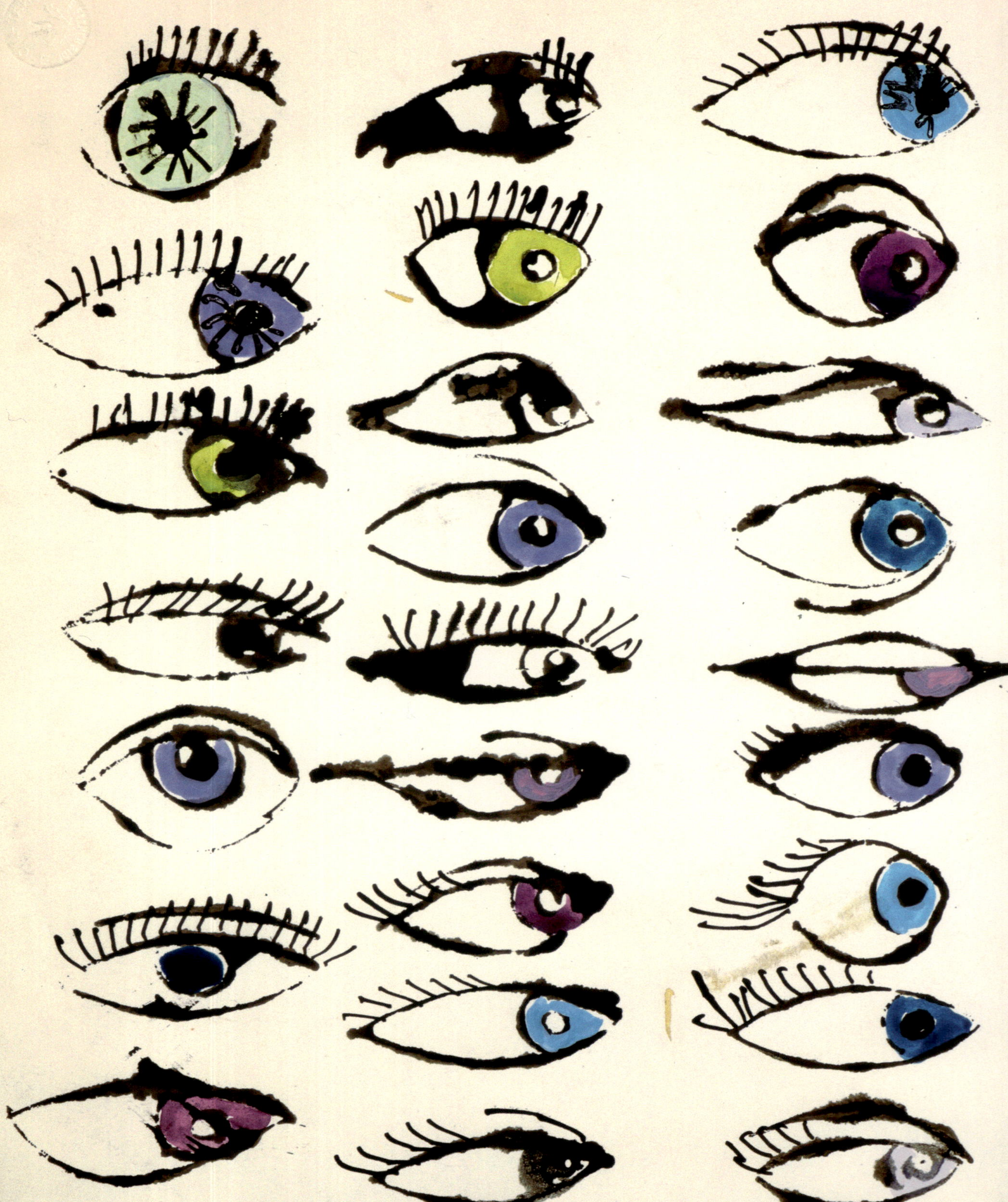

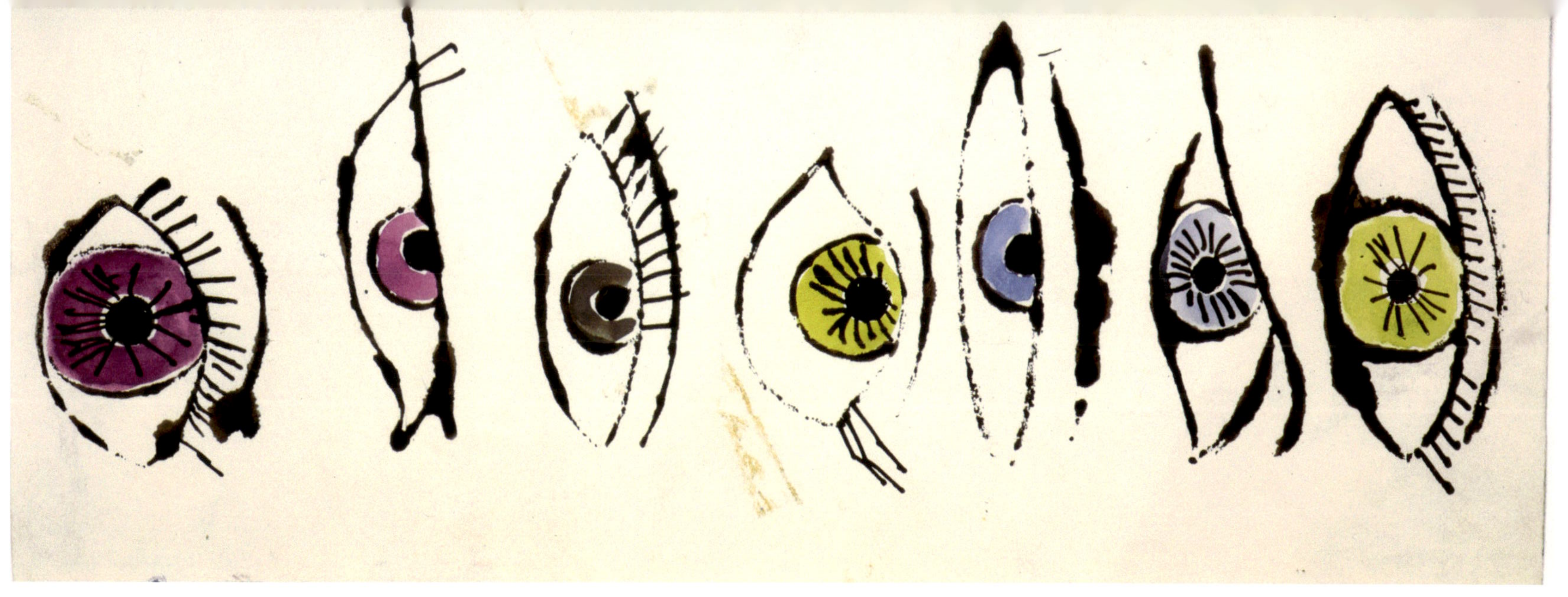

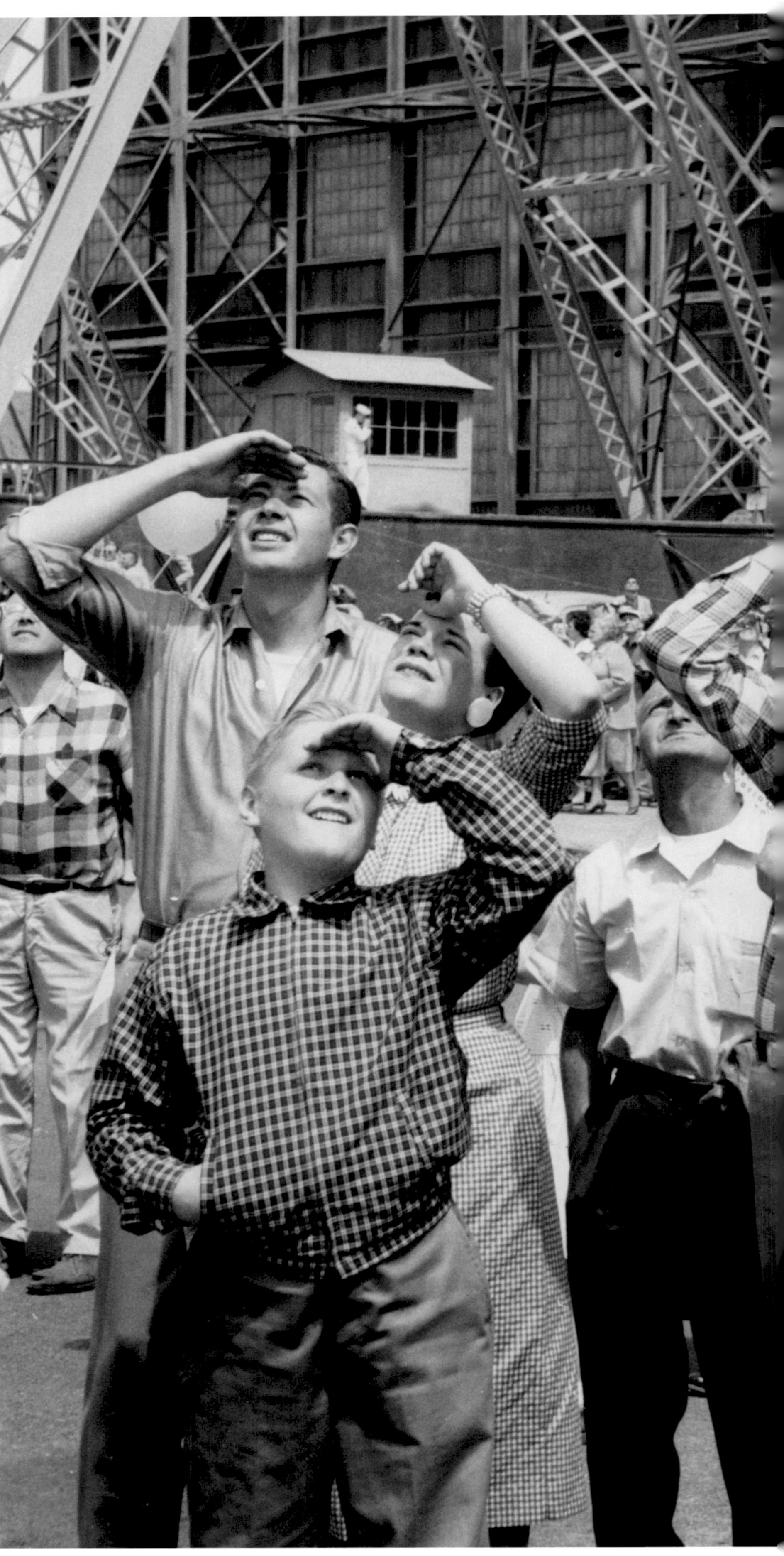

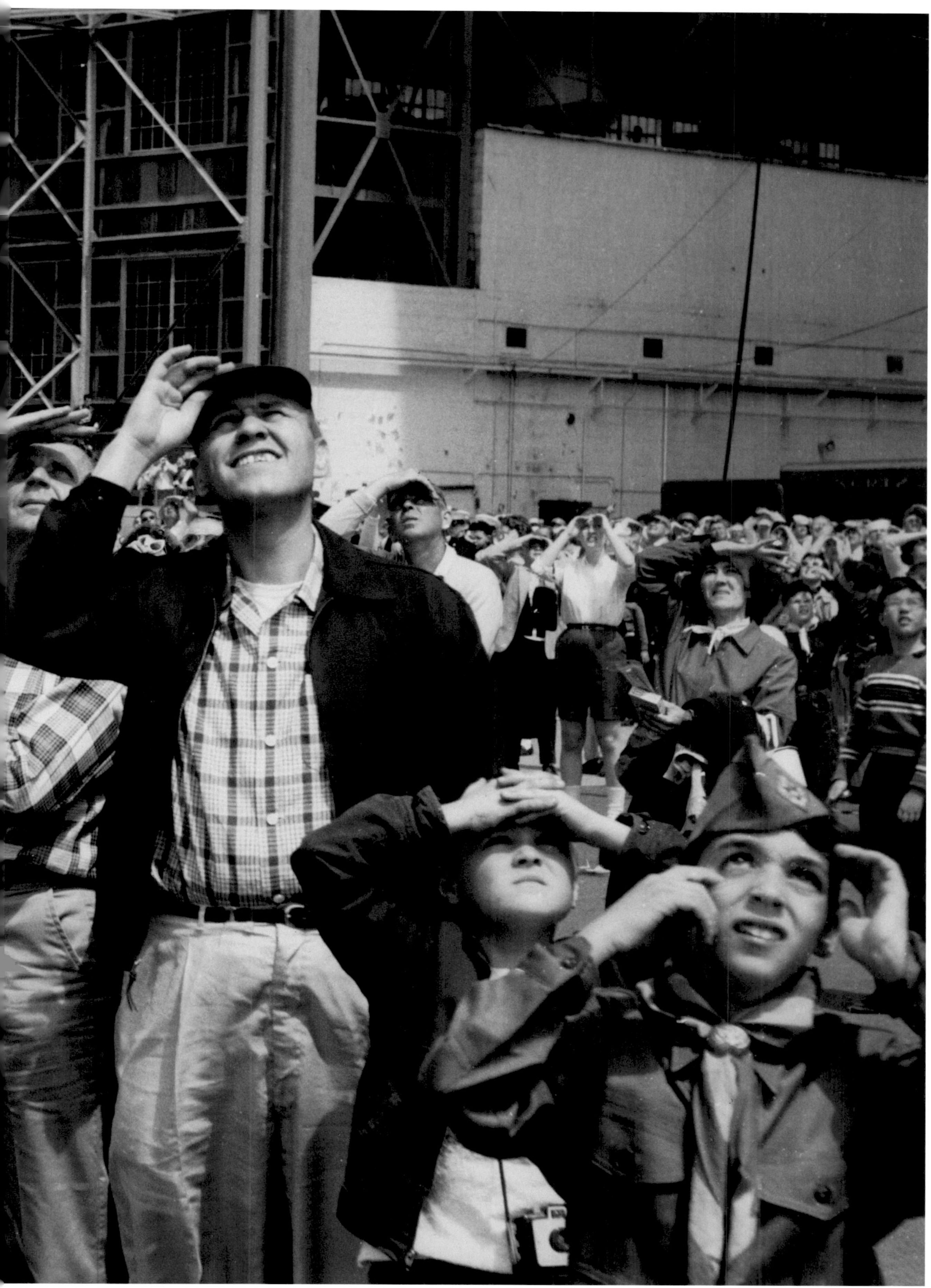

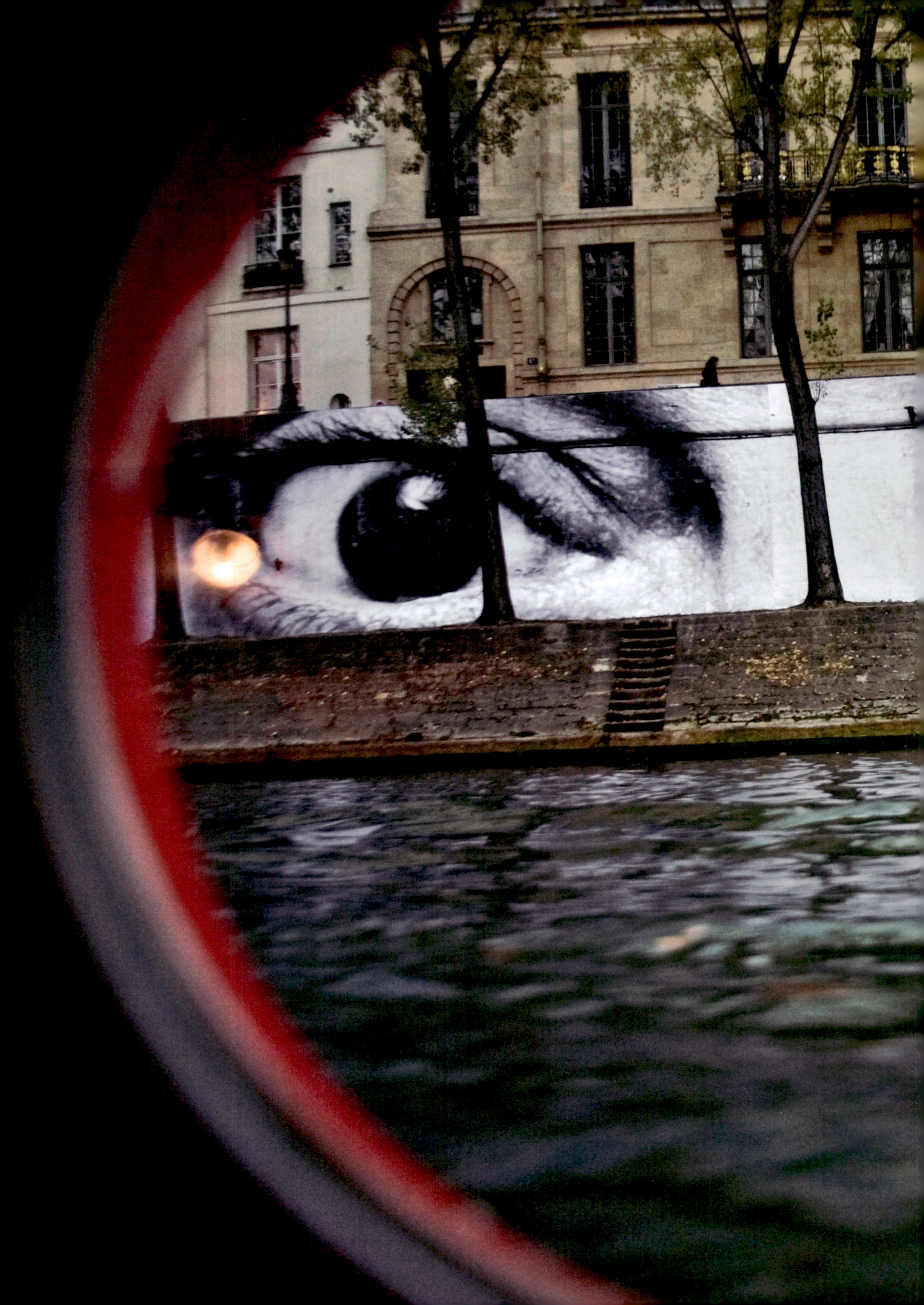

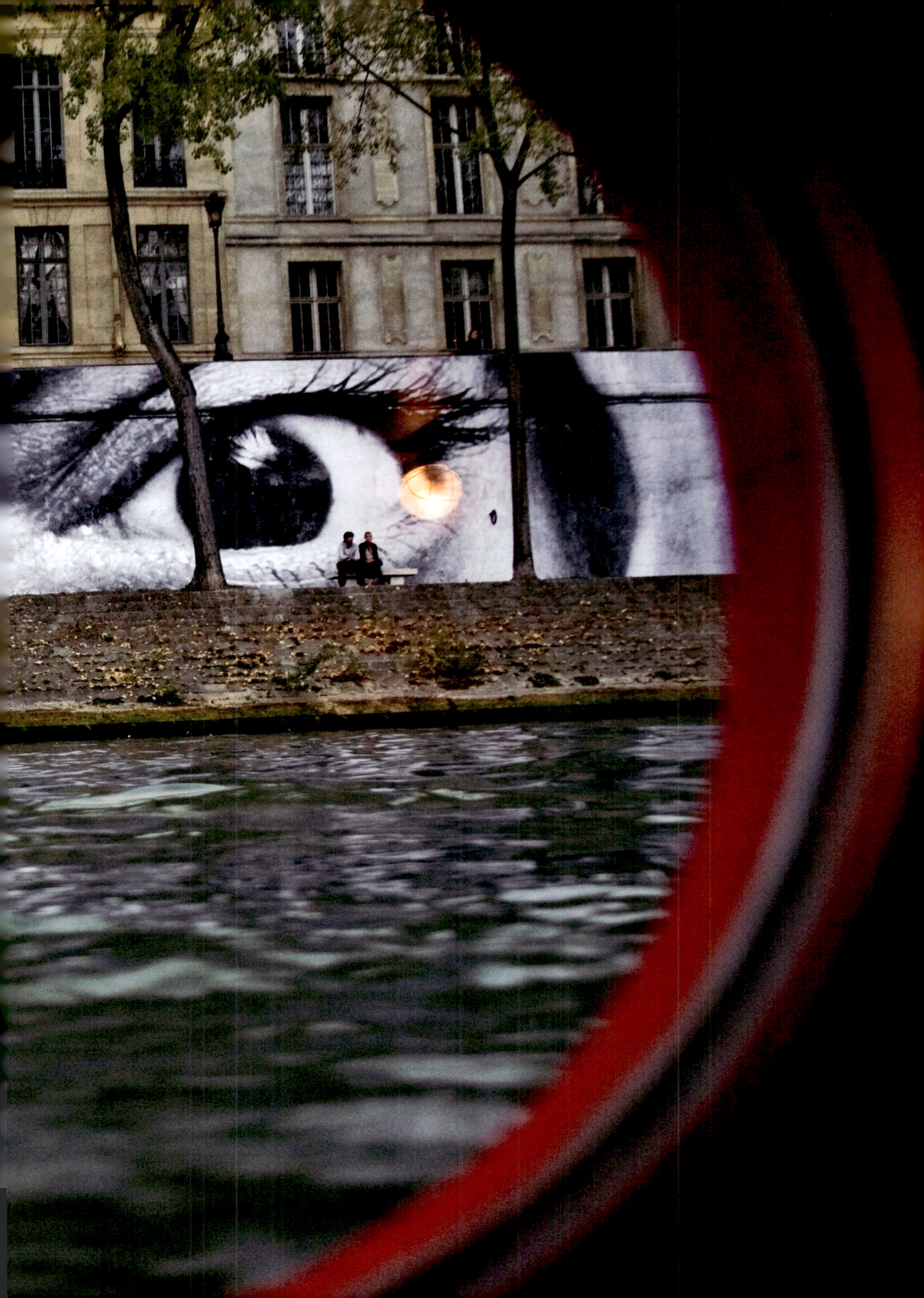

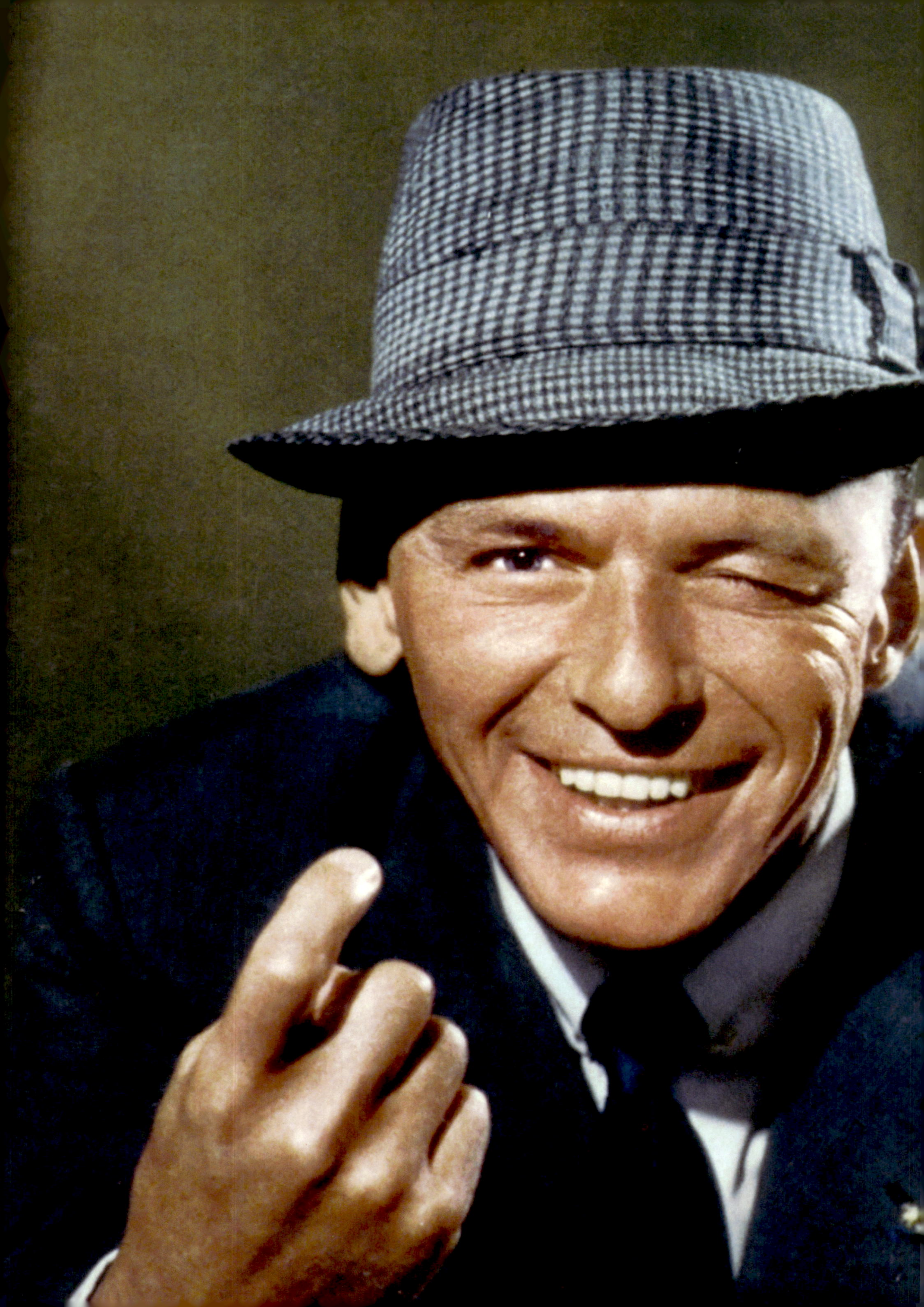

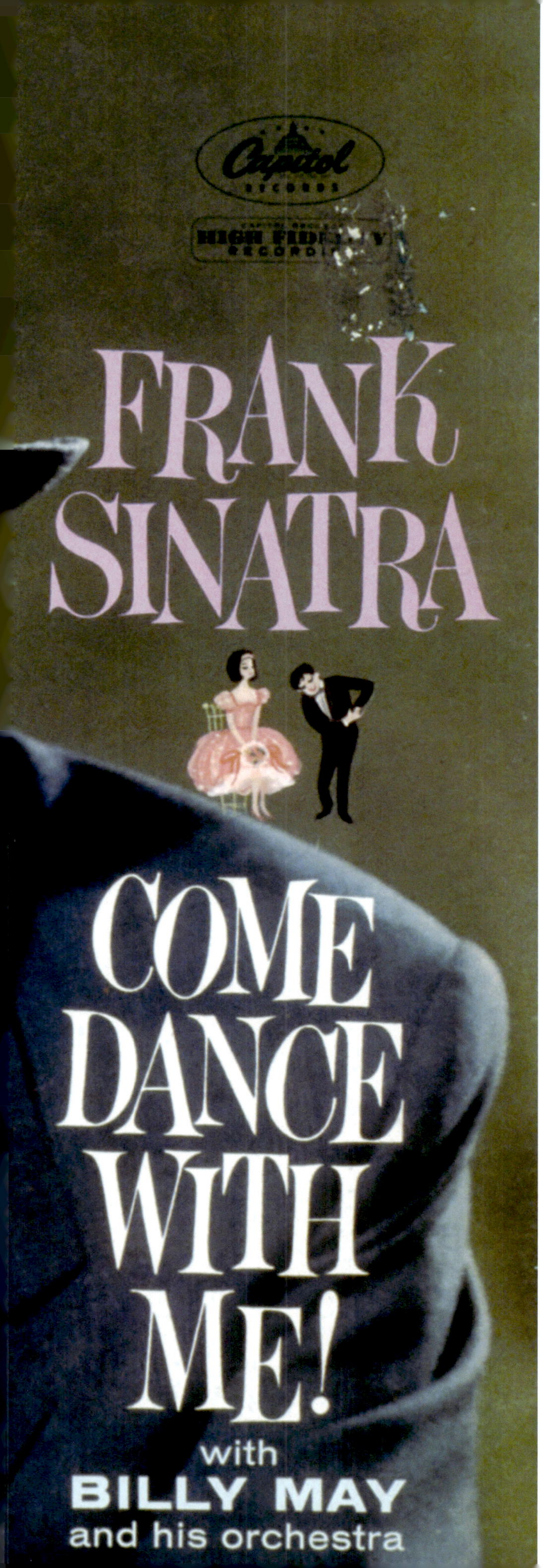

Capitol RECORDS

HIGH FIDELITY RECORDING

FRANK SINATRA

COME DANCE WITH ME!

with BILLY MAY and his orchestra

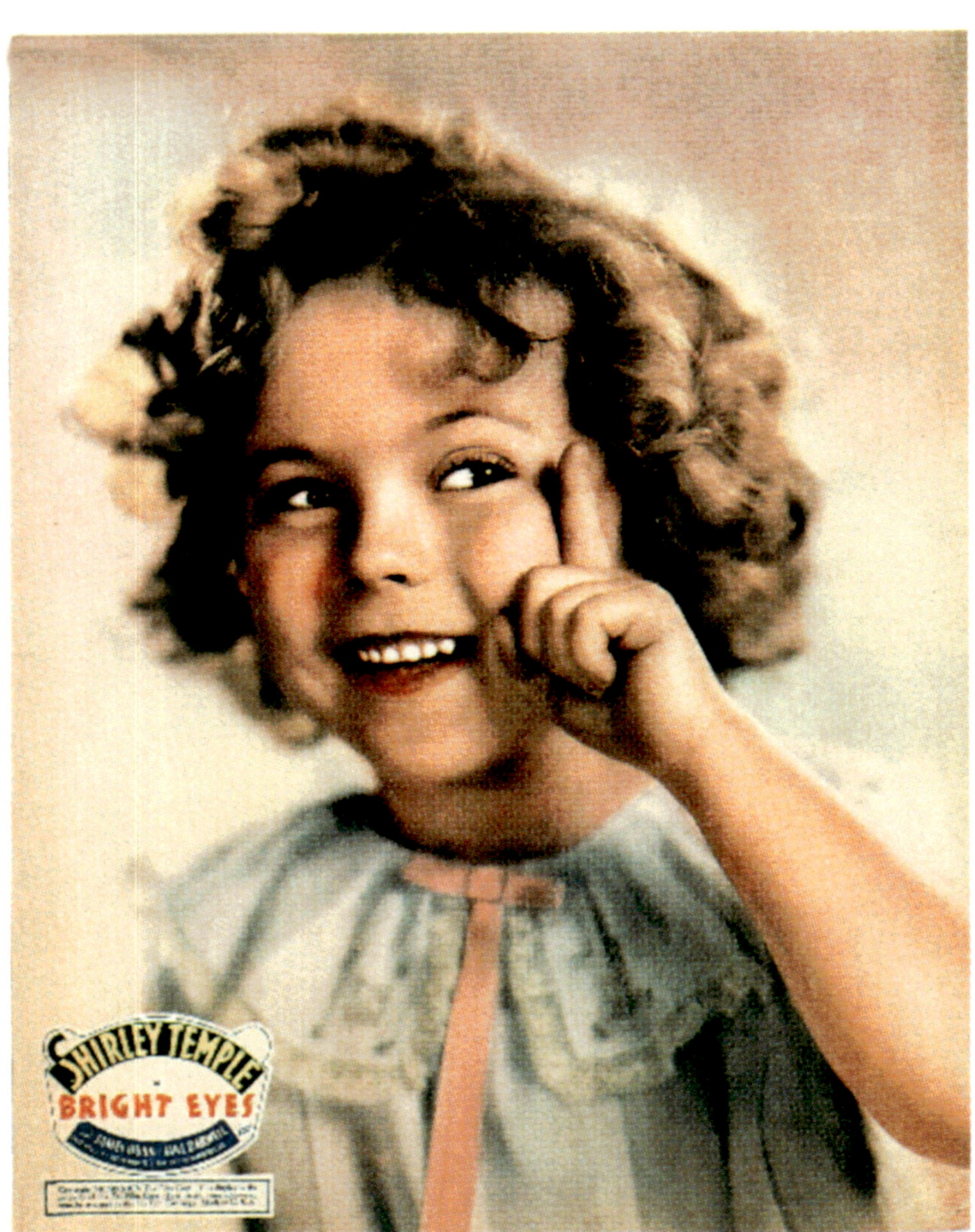
SHIRLEY TEMPLE
BRIGHT EYES

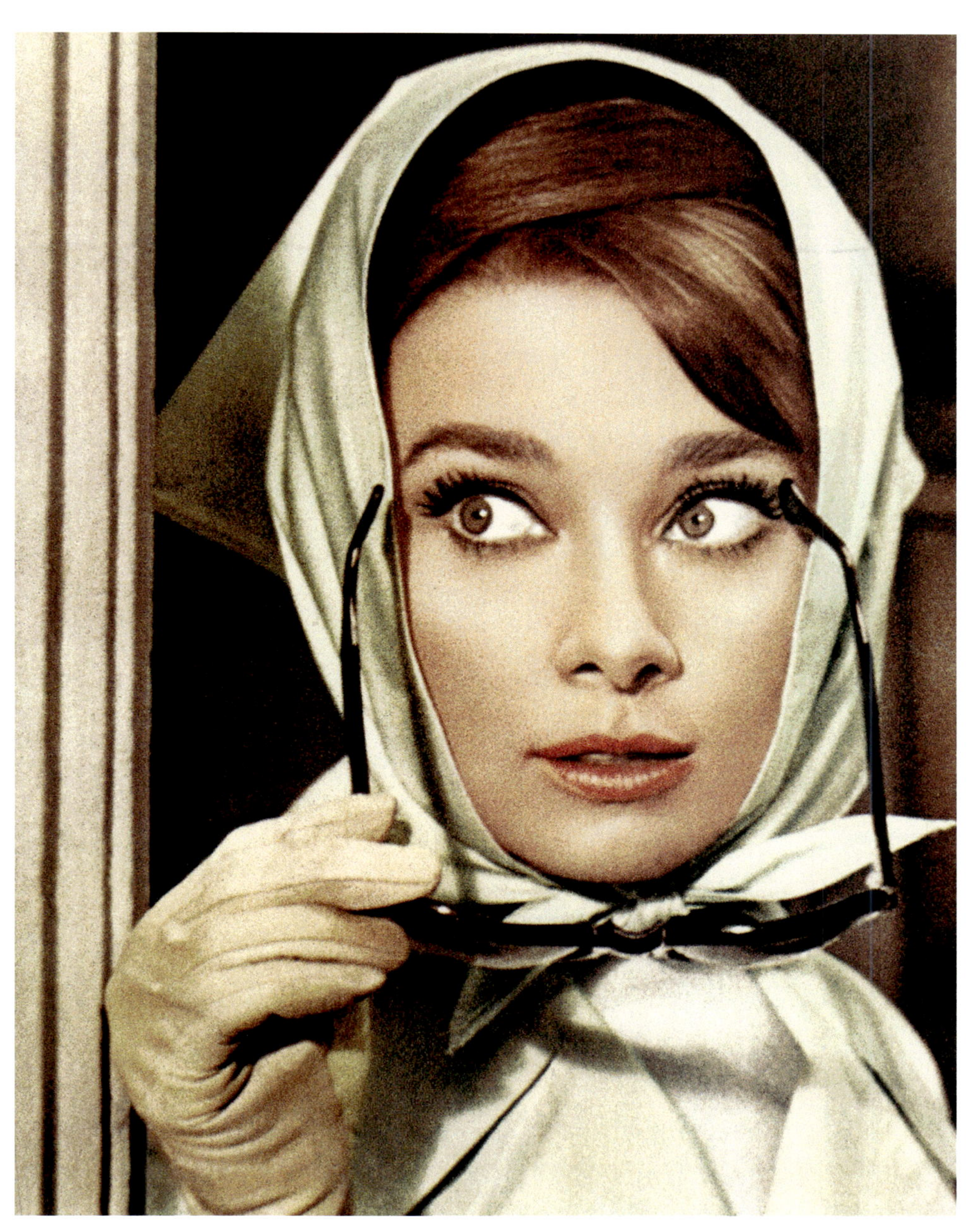

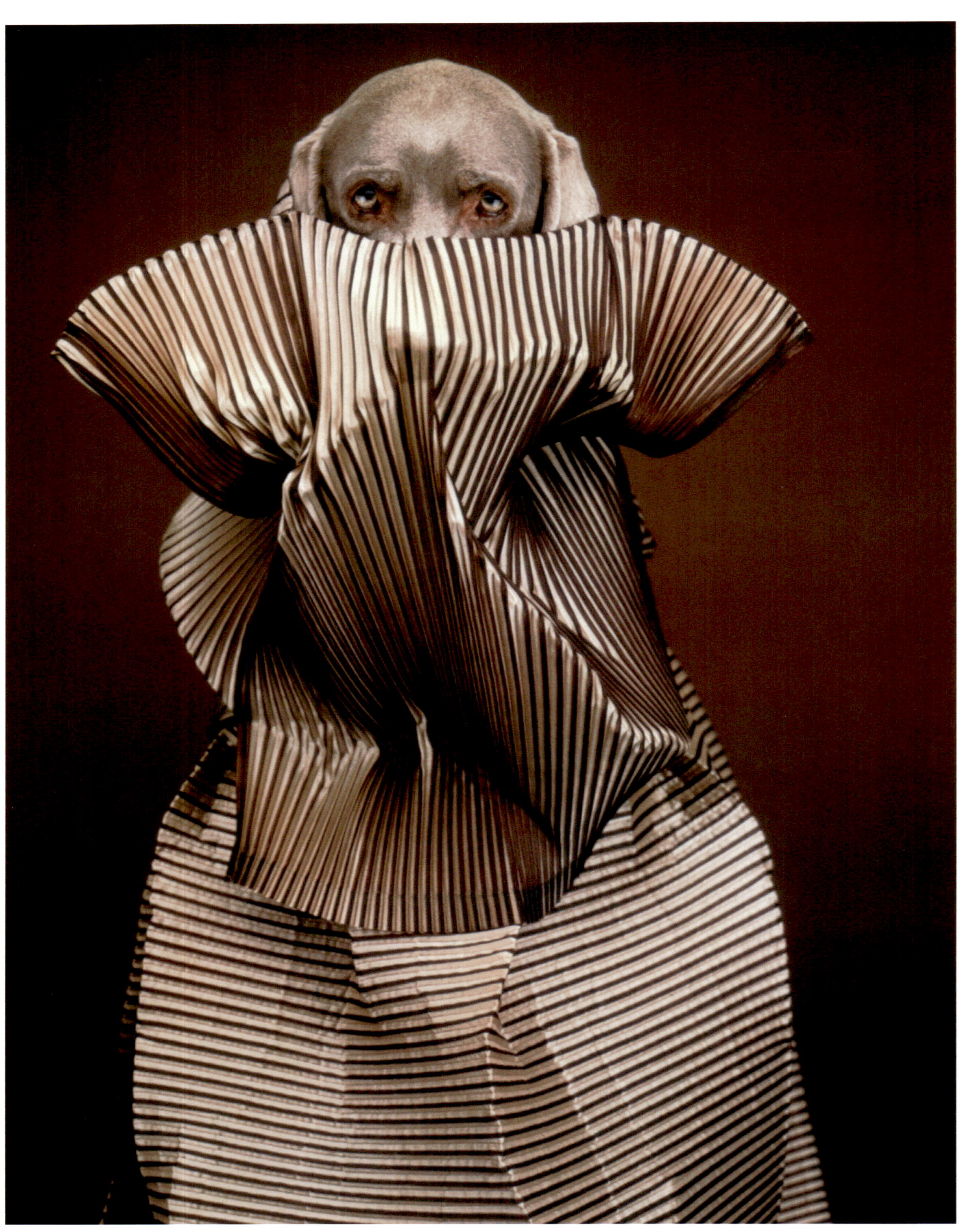

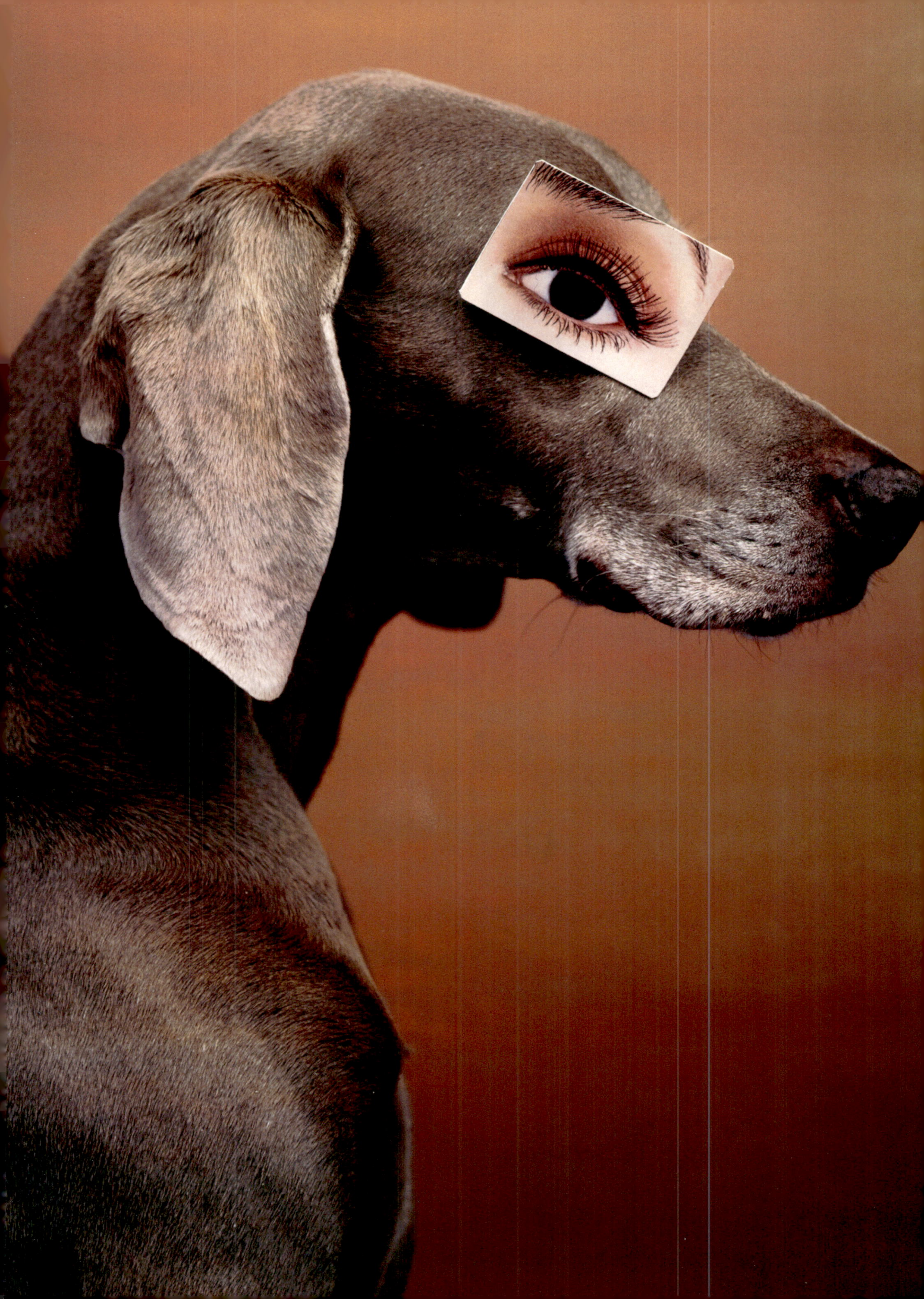

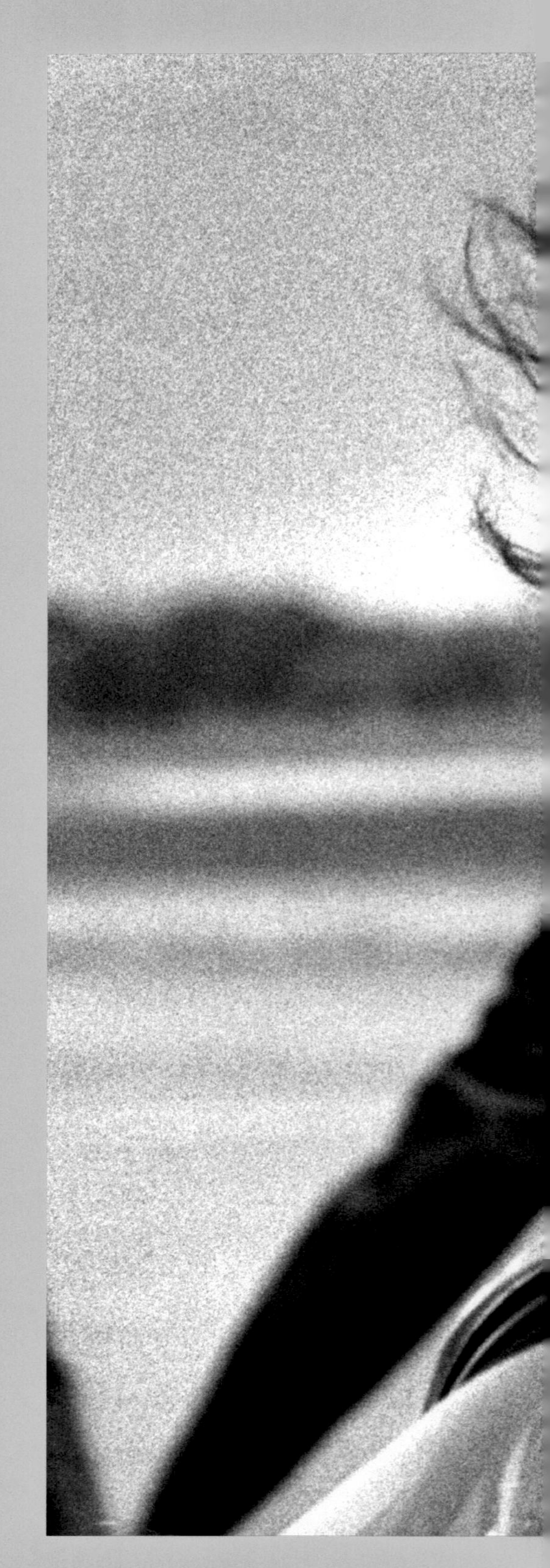

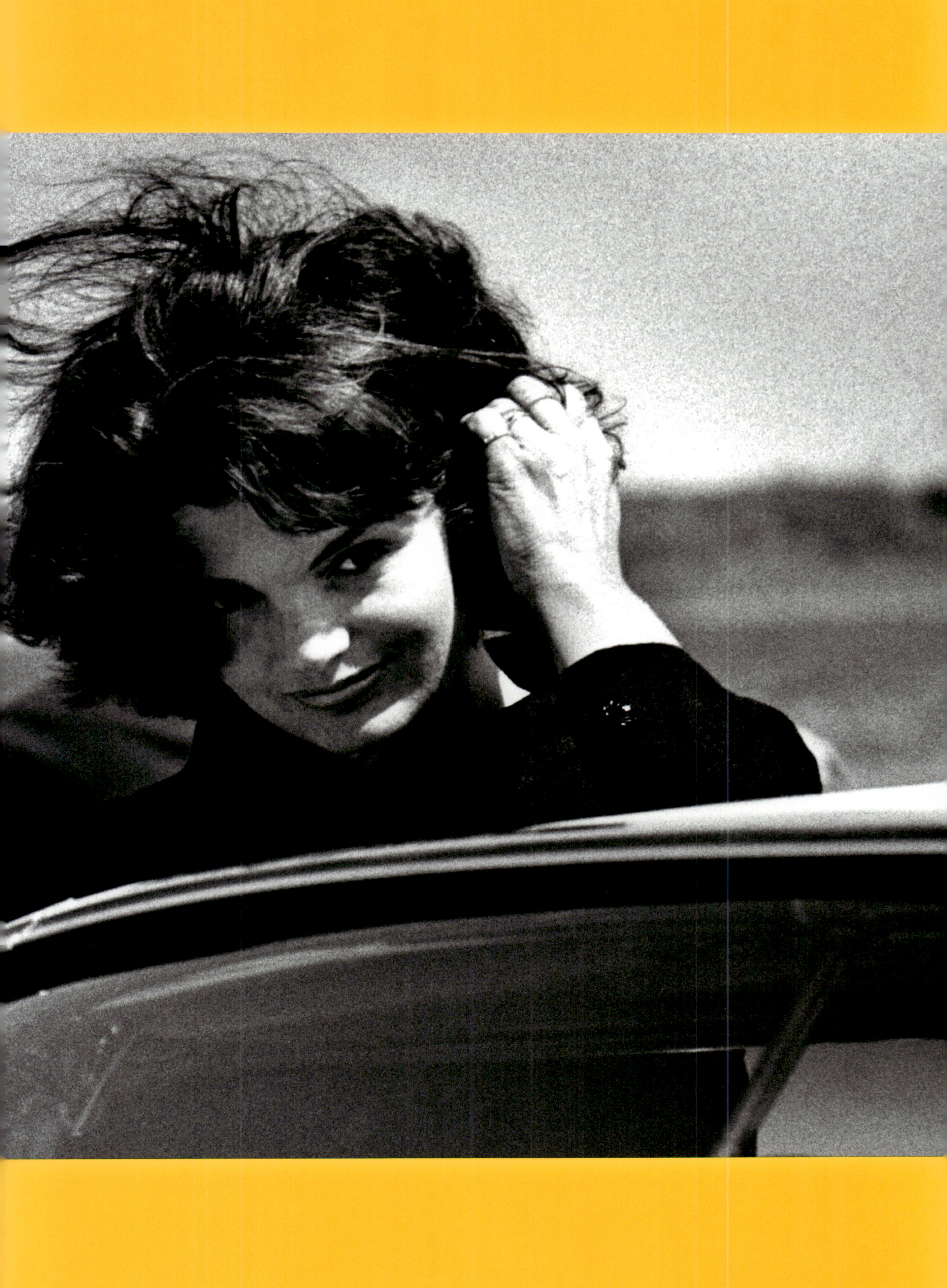

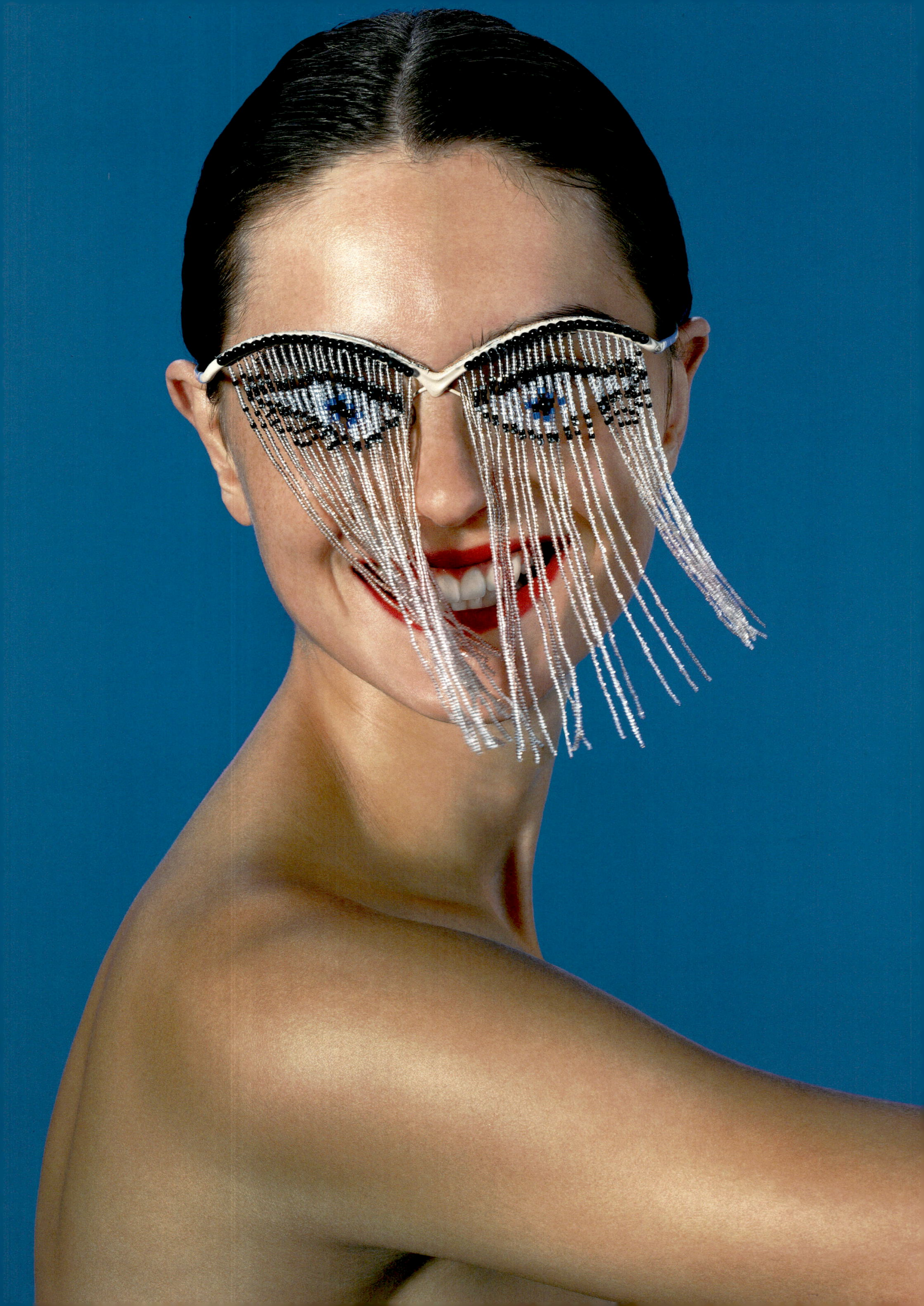

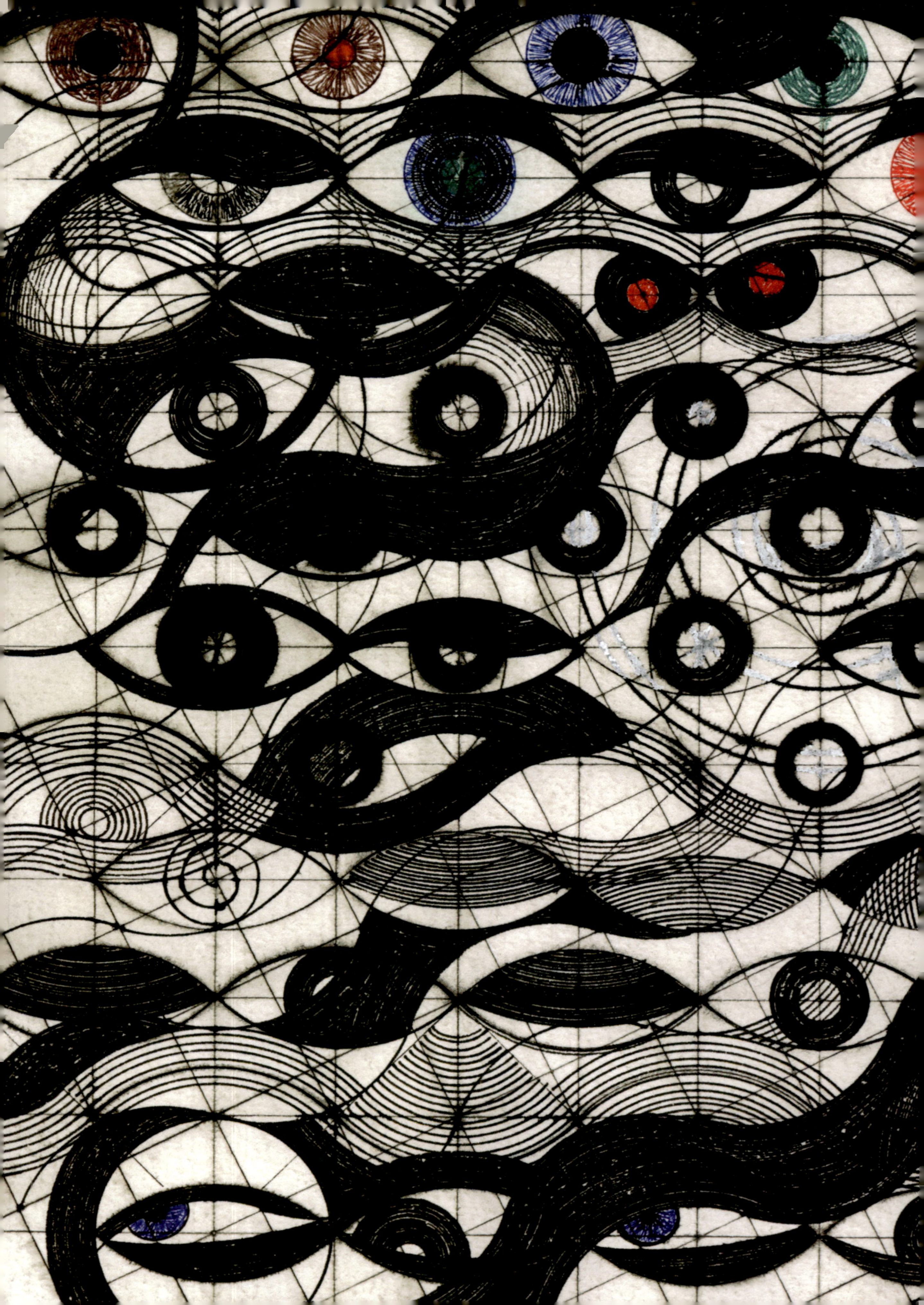

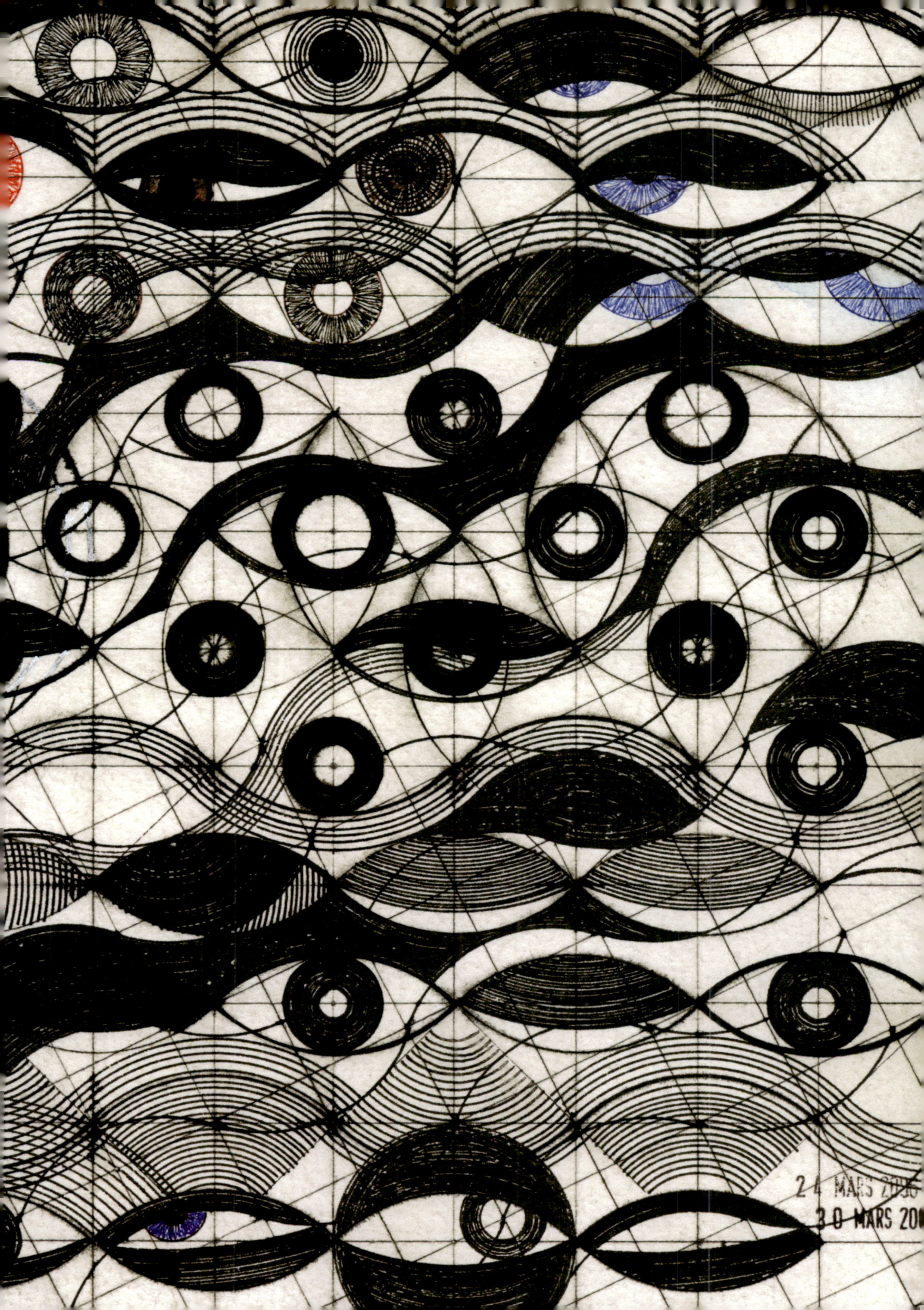
2 4 MARS 2006
3 0 MARS 20

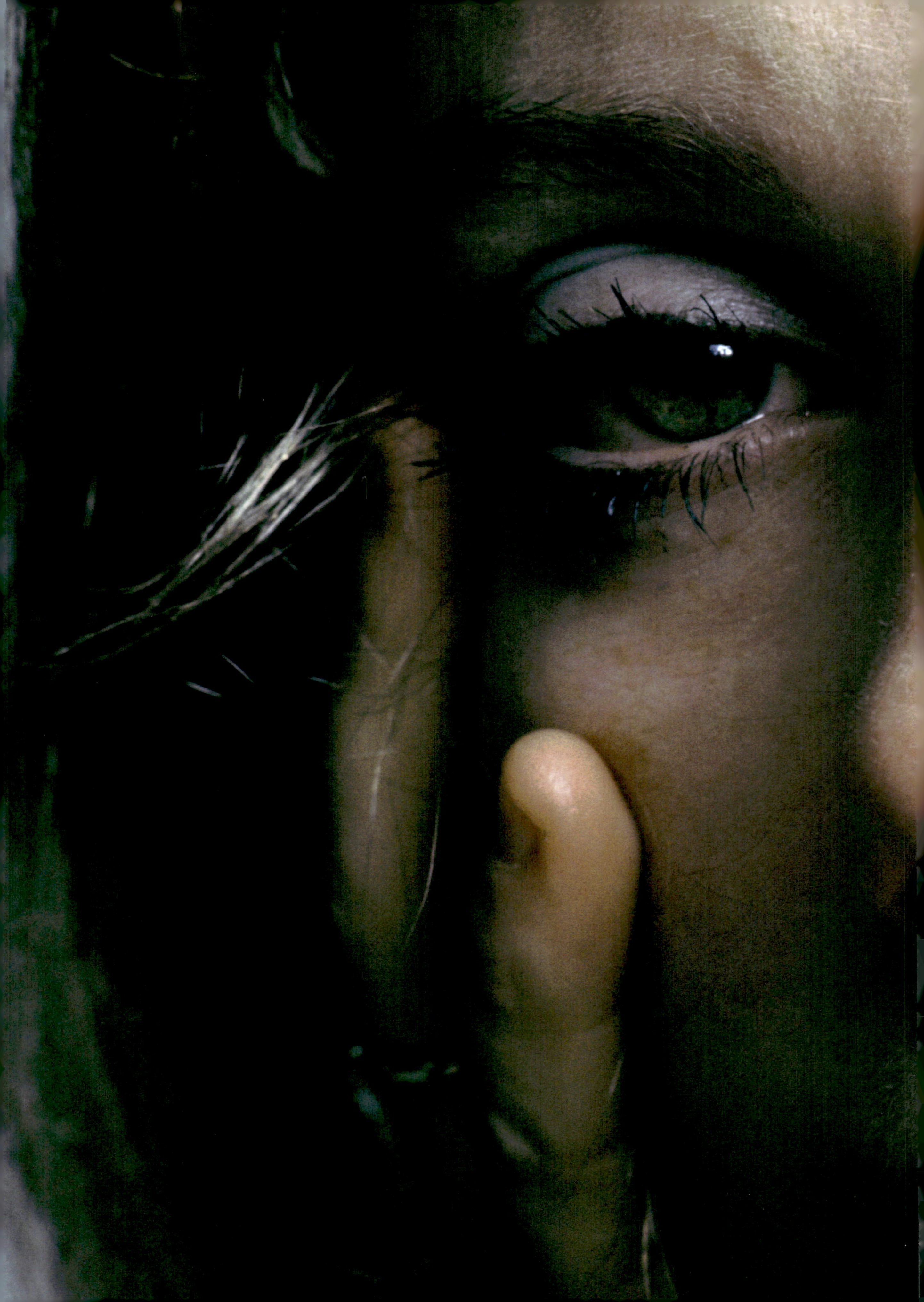

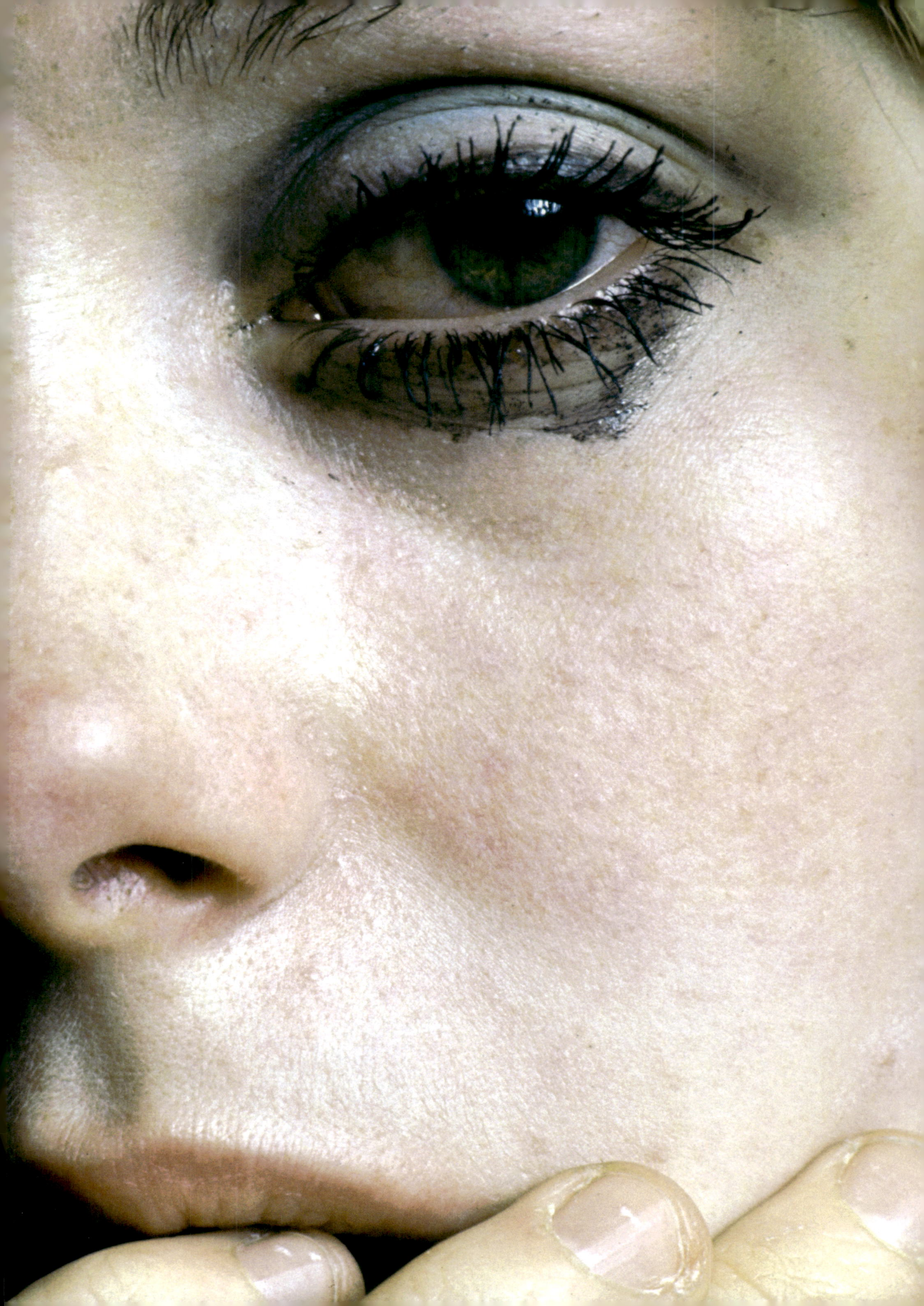

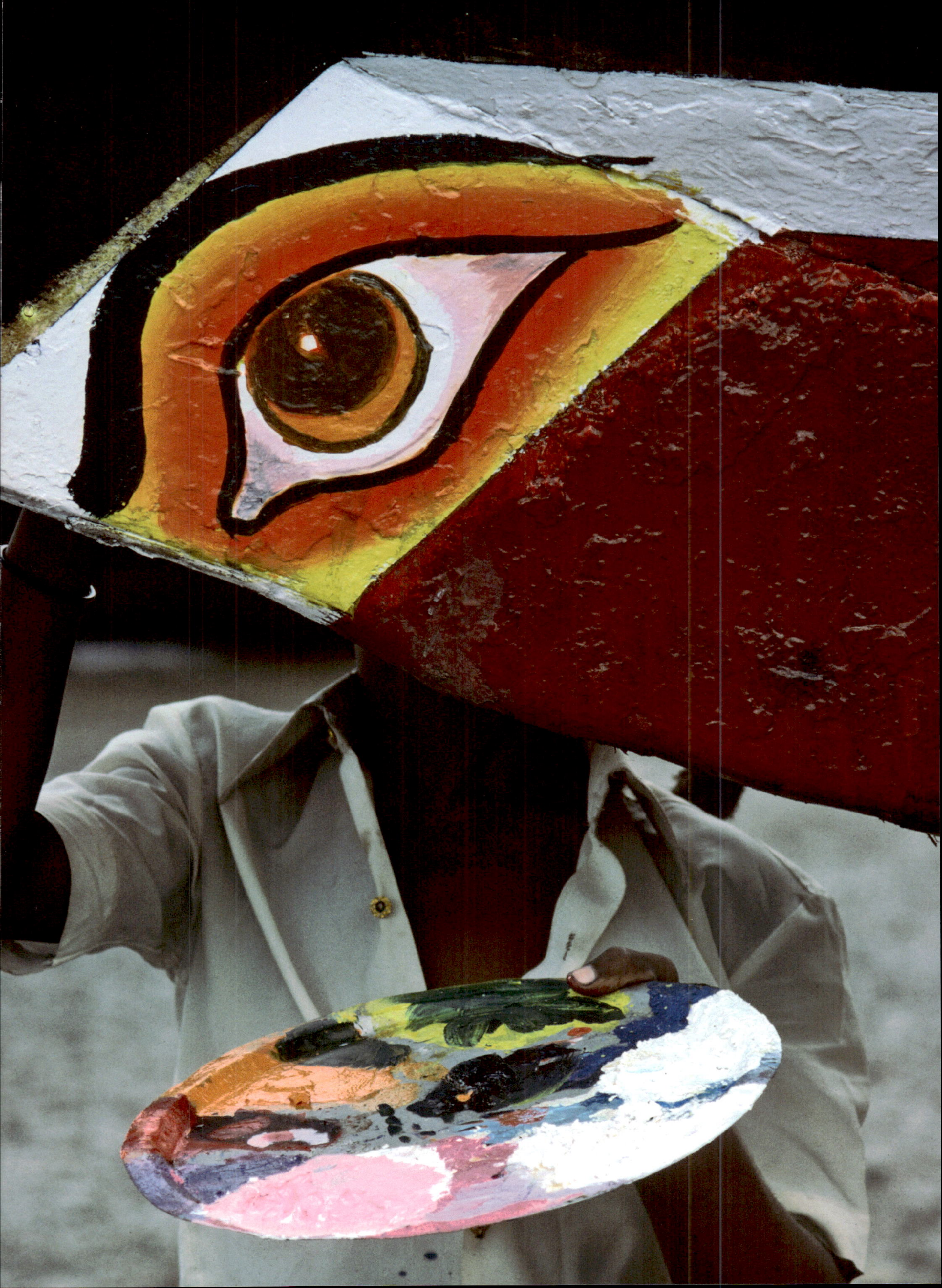

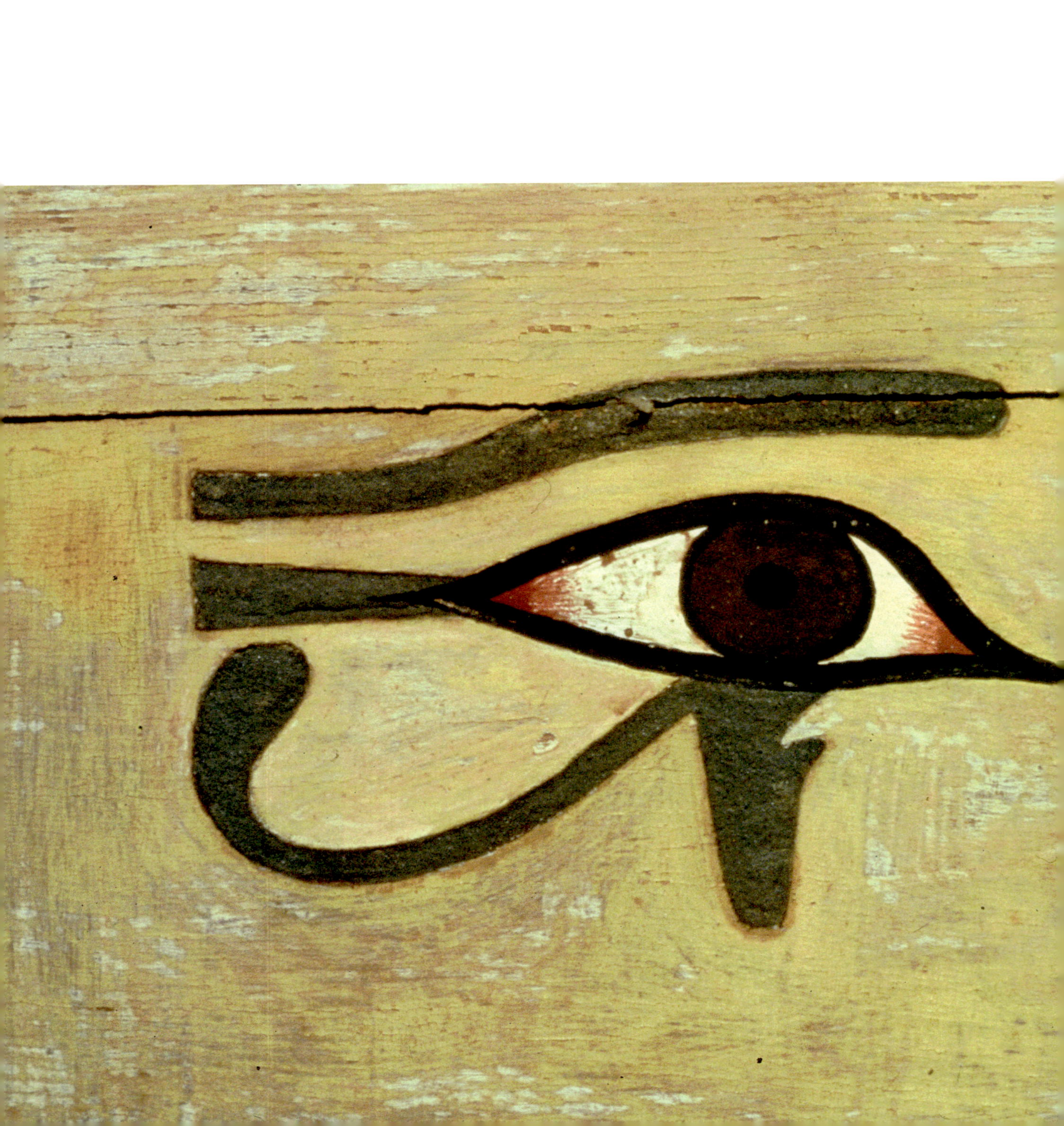

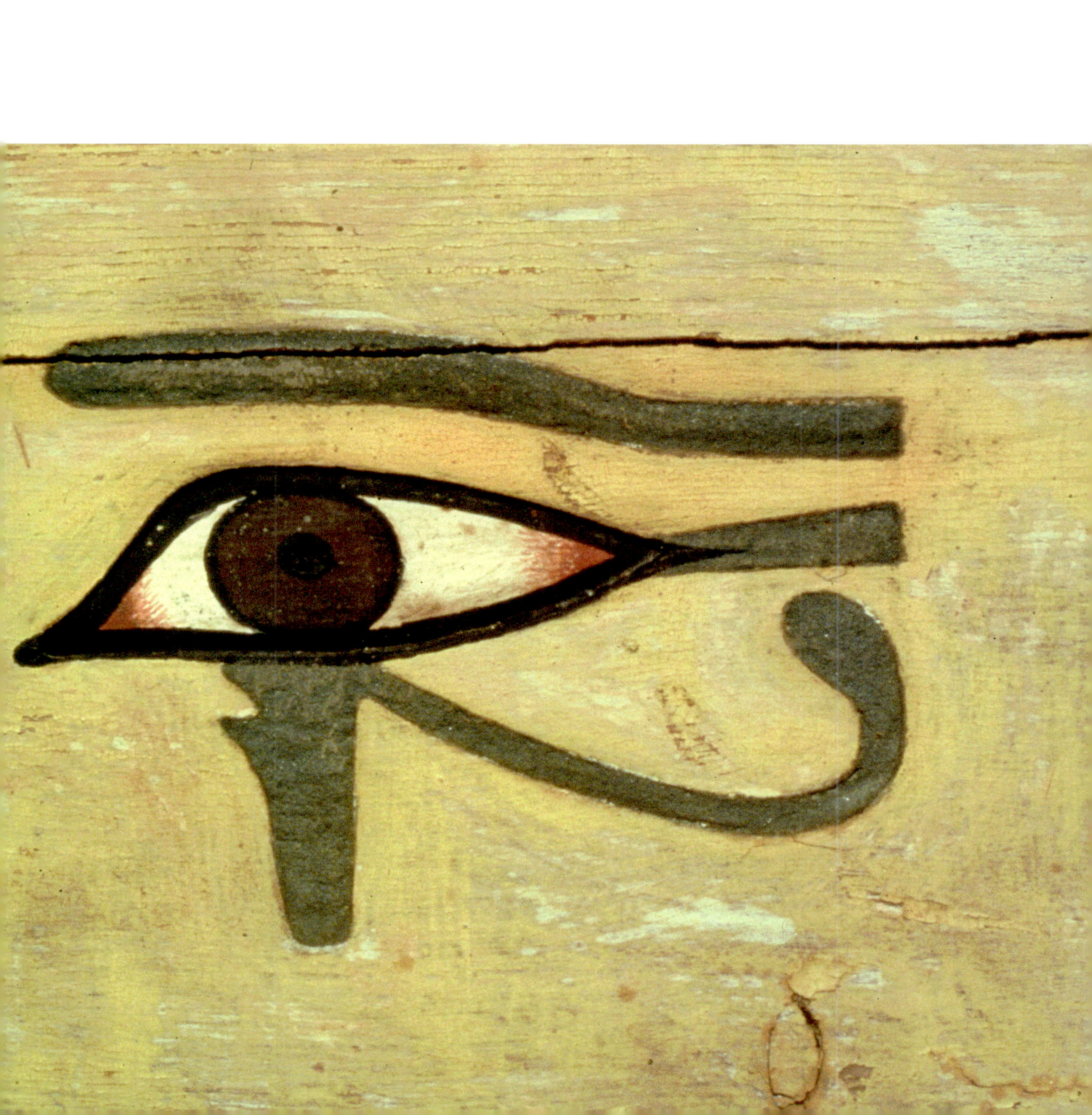

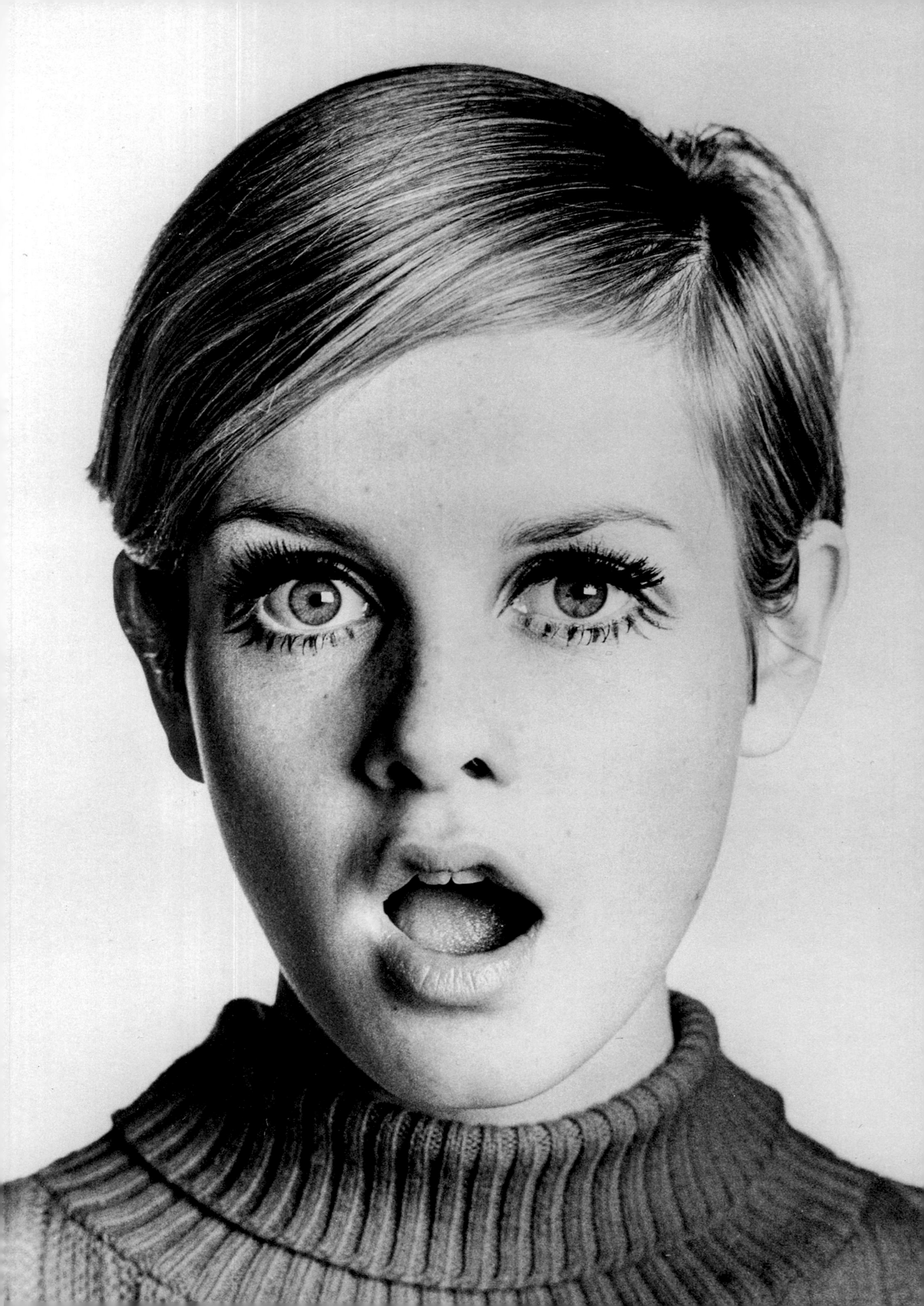

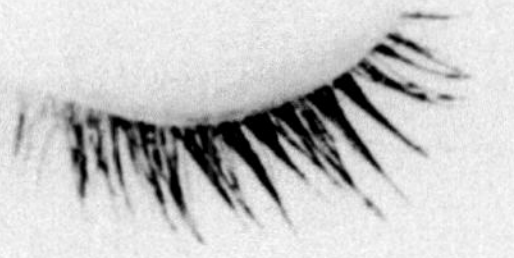

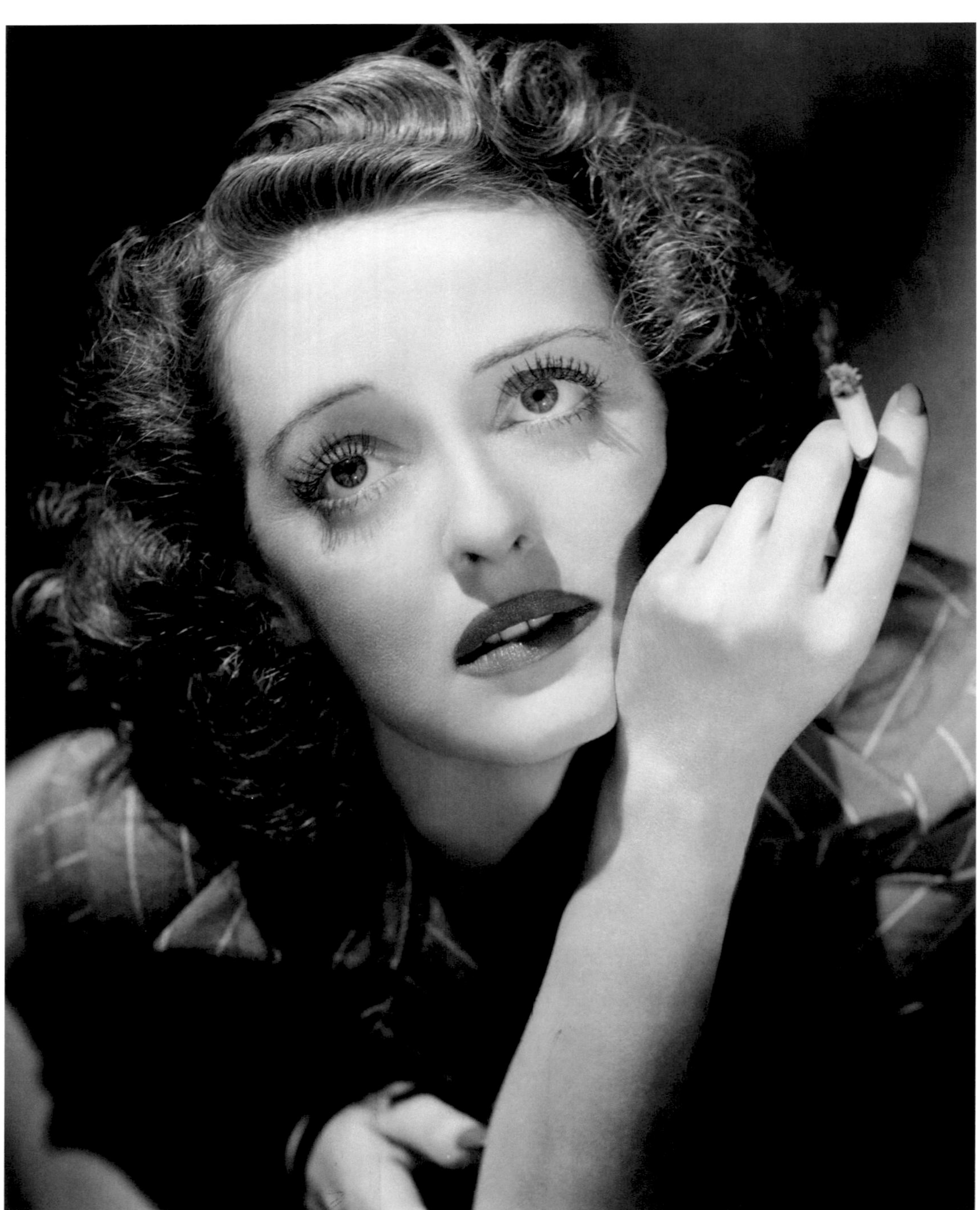

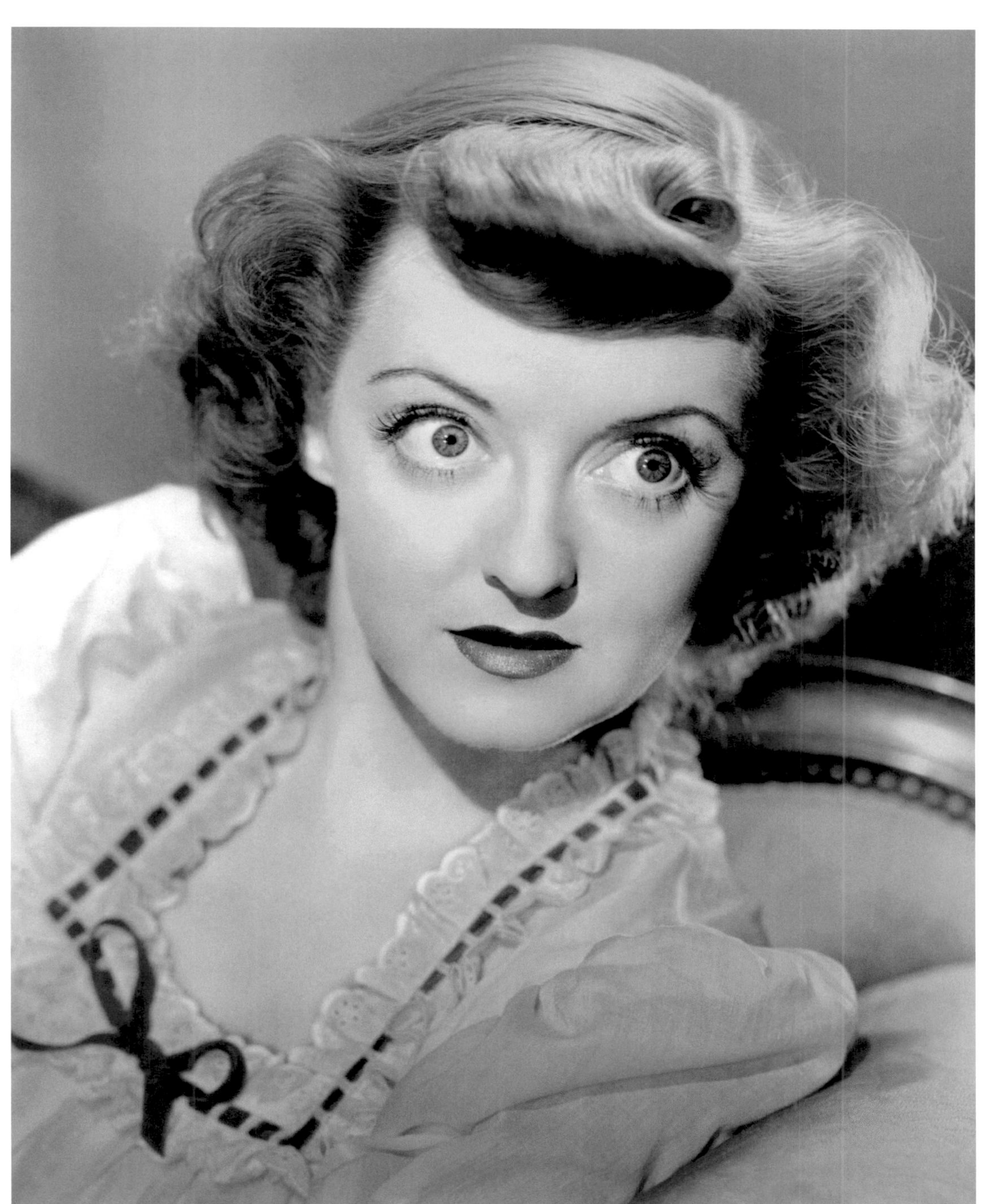

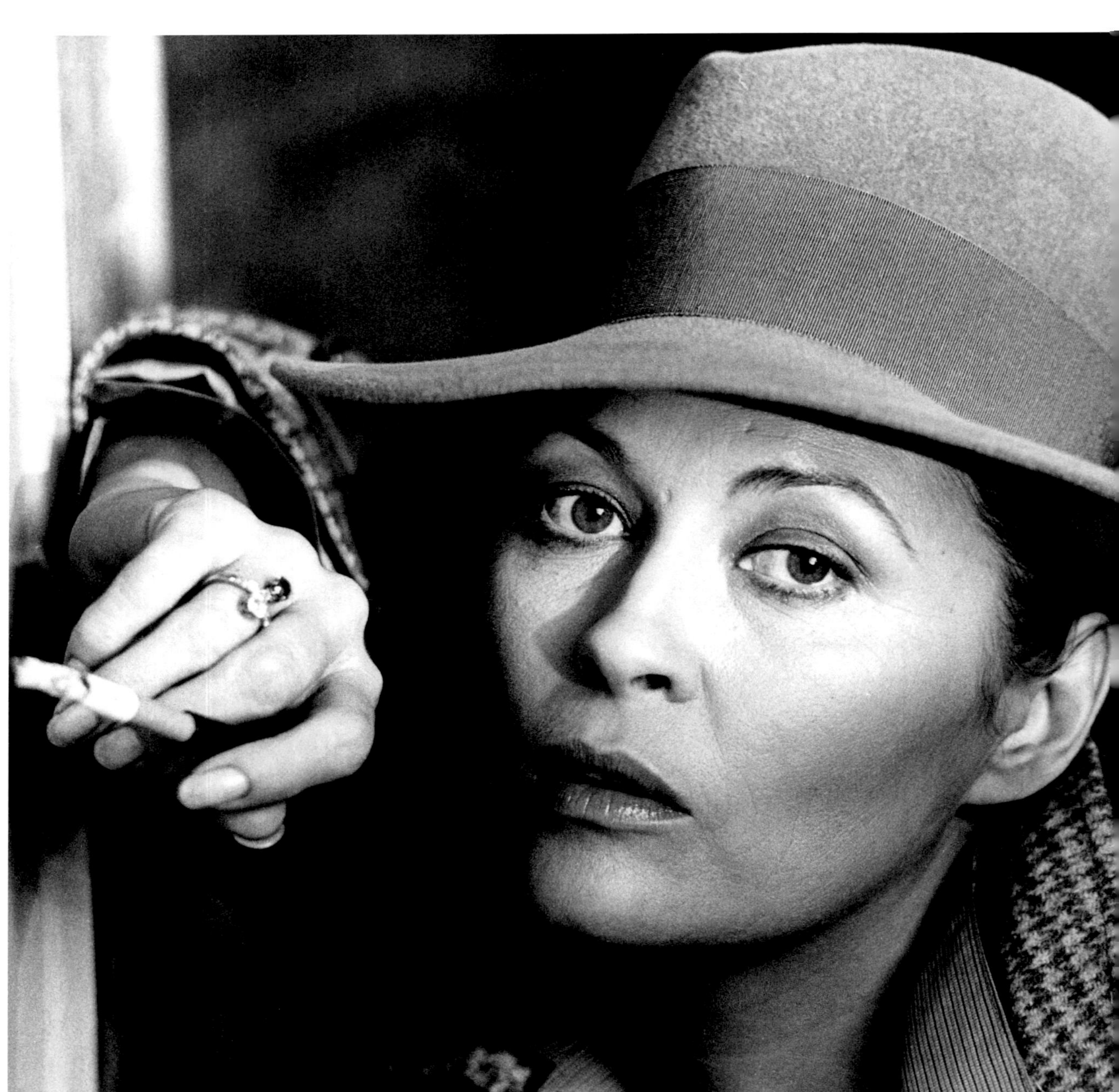

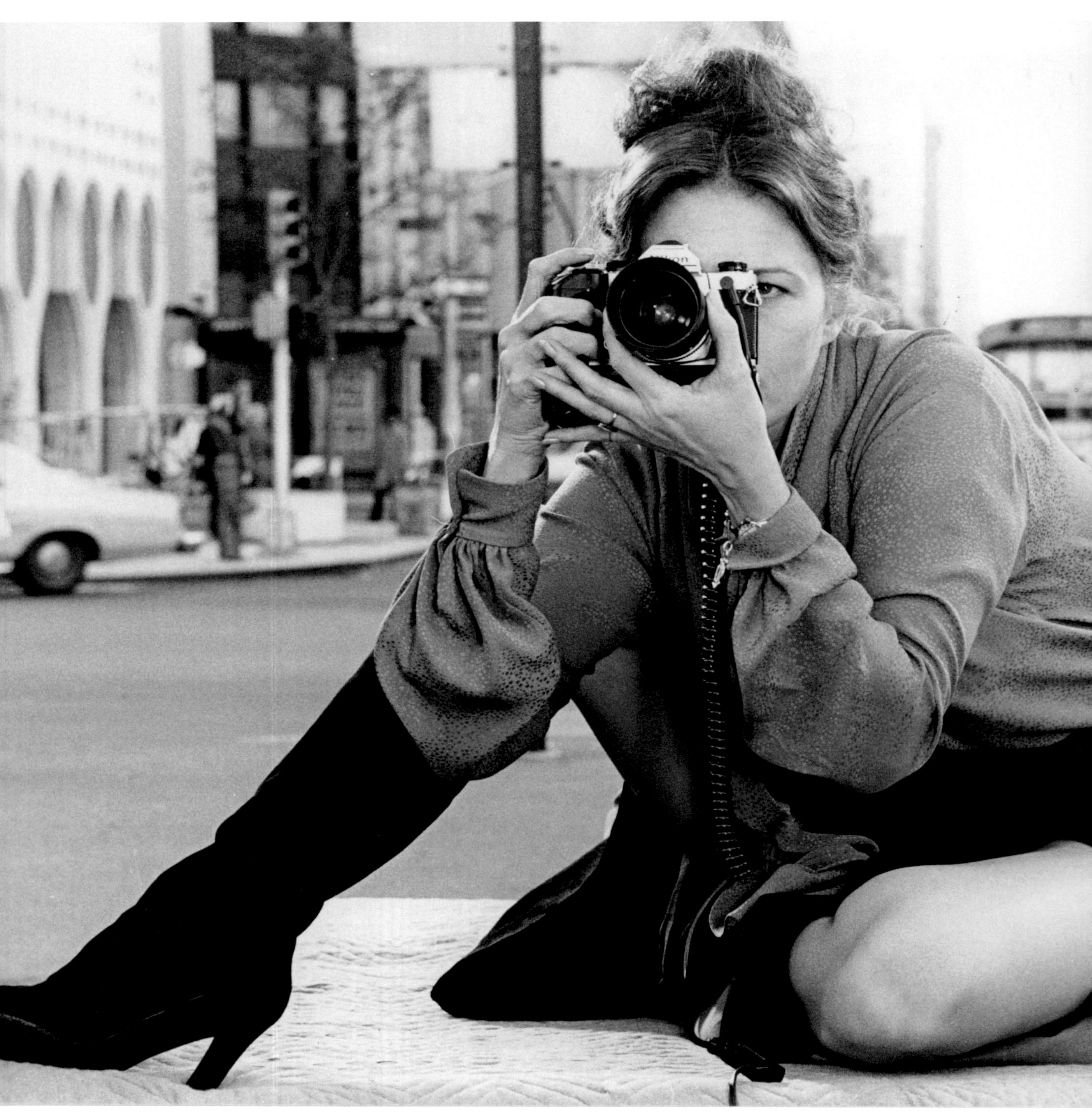

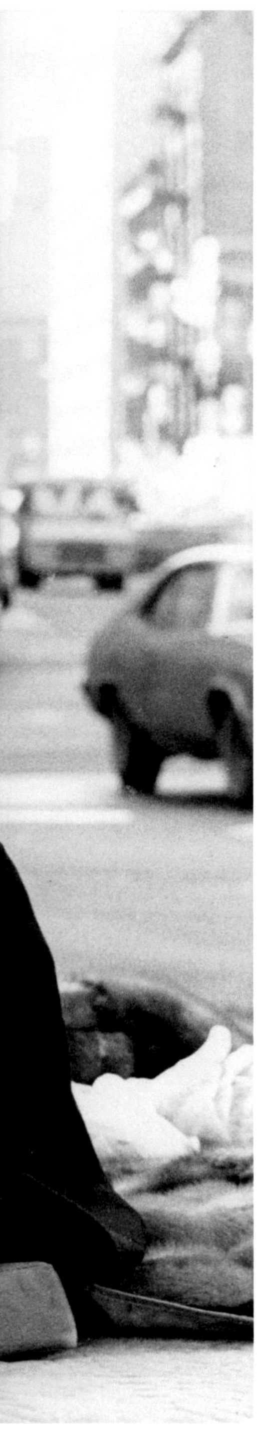

Acknowledgements

I am forever grateful to:
My amazing husband Stanley..."I Only Have Eyes For You."
One fabulous song for one fabulous man!!

My beautiful children,
Samantha, David, Jessie, Ben, Noah, and Lizzie!

Craig Cohen, Sarina Finkelstein Leventi, Ormond Gigli, and Christian John Wikane....Your inspiration and encouragement got me to the finish line... Book five, wow!

The East Hampton Library and Dennis Fabiszak.
Thank you for your support!

Last, but not least, my incredible friends and family:
Joni and Christopher Fischer, Deborah and Tom Sayles, Deneen and Ray King, Helen and Andrew Sheinman, Mia and Giles Masters, Bruce Sudano, Denise Eppolito and Eddie Hokenson, Georgia and Gerry Curatola, Randi and Jeff Guyton, Adam Paige, Beverly Paige, Dag Arne Kristensen and Christian Wallis, Ken Moore and Keith Scott, Amanda and Abner Ramirez, Mimi and Rick Dohler, Brooklyn and Mike McGlaflin, Eva and Vincent Giagni, Michele Eppolito, Yvette and Andy Gellis, Allison Wiedman, Bonnie and Steve Blacker, Pauline and Milt Zablow, Jean Lee Yamner, Elycia and Brad Kaplan, Paul Orenstein and Rene Vazquez, Rosemary Peck, Minnie Cho, Robert Risko,
Donna Summer Sudano—Forever!

My backup singers:
Mika Supato
Sadah Saltzman
Aida Angjeli
Izabela Dziak
Yasmine Djerradine
Nikky Ray

The author's royalties will be donated to the East Hampton Library

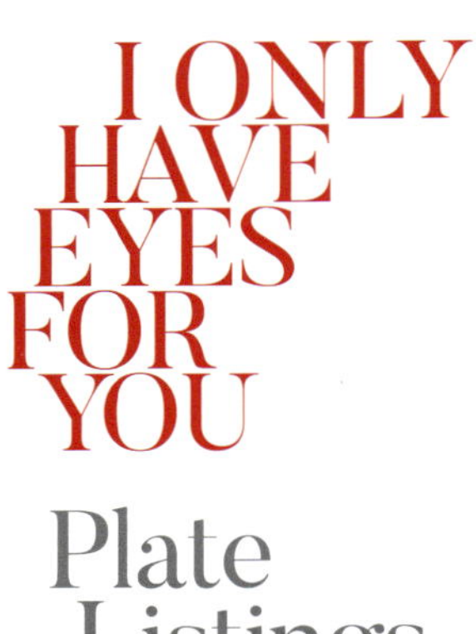

Plate Listings

Front jacket Sophia Loren, Rome, 1955 by Ormond Gigli © Ormond Gigli
Pages 2-3 "Glass Tears," Man Ray, photograph, 1932. © ARS, NY. Banque d'Images, ADAGP/ Art Resource, NY
Page 6 Formally attired audience sporting 3D glasses during opening night screening of film *Bwana Devil*, the first full-length color 3D motion picture, J. R. Eyerman, Los Angeles, California, December 1952. © J. R. Eyerman/The LIFE Picture Collection/Getty Images
Pages 10-11 The sun of the Japanese flag painted on a girl's forehead, Thomas Hoepker, 1977. © Thomas Hoepker, Tokyo, Japan/Magnum Photos
Page 13 George Clooney, Martin Schoeller, 2008. © Martin Schoeller/AUGUST
Page 14 "Kettledrummer," Paul Klee, 1940. © Paul Klee, De Agostini Editore/ Bridgeman Images
Page 15 "Scherzo di Follia," Pierre-Louis Pierson, © The Metropolitan Museum of Art, Image source: Art Resource, NY
Pages 16-17 Malcolm McDowell as Alex Delarge in Stanley Kubrick's *A Clockwork Orange*, 1971. © Getty Images
Pages 18-19 Young newlyweds at the Butlins Ocean Hotel in Saltdean, nicknamed the "Honeymoon Hotel," Peter Purdy, UK, c.1955. © BIPs/Getty Images
Pages 20-21 "Crying Girl," Roy Lichtenstein, 1964. © Roy Lichtenstein
Page 22 June Pickney, Stan Wayman, 1960. © Stan Wayman/The LIFE Picture Collection
Page 23 Model, James Macari, 2014. © James Macari
Pages 24-25 Philippe Halsman, 1938. © Philippe Halsman / Magnum Photos
Page 26 "Head of a man with straw hat," Pablo Picasso, 1971. © Pablo Picasso/ Bridgeman Images
Page 28 Guy Bourdin © Guy Bourdin Estate, 2018
Page 29 © Herbert Matter/Vogue Conde Nast
Pages 30-31 "Mona Lisa," Leonardo da Vinci, c.1503-17. © RMN-Grand Palais / Art Resource, NY
Page 32 Michael Douglas, Martin Schoeller, 2013. © Martin Schoeller/AUGUST
Page 33 Natalie Portman as seen in Darren Aronofsky's *Black Swan*, 2010. © Fox Searchlight, Ronald Grant Archive/Mary Evans/Everett Collection
Pages 34-35 © Patrick Zachmann, France 2013 / Magnum Photos
Pages 36-37 CBS logo designer William Golden, 1952. © Bill Warnecke/CBS Photo Archive/ Getty Images
Page 38 Tian Yi, Chinese opera performer, Mario Testino, China, 2013. © Mario Testino, Art Partner
Pages 40-41 "The False Mirror," Rene Magritte, 1935. © ARS, NY; Banque d'Images, ADAGP/ Art Resource, NY
Pages 42-43 Helen Evans and three sailors at Rockefeller Center, 1955. © Ed Clarity/NY Daily News Archive/Getty Images
Pages 44-45 "American Girl in Italy," Ruth Orkin, Italy, 1951. © 1952, 1980 Ruth Orkin
Pages 46-47 "The Italian Turn," Mario de Biasi, Italy, 1954. © MondadoriPortfolio. Mario De Biasi
Pages 48-49 Model, 1969. © Keystone/Getty Images
Pages 50-51 Captain Jacques-Yves Cousteau on the set of *Le Monde Du Silence*, 1956. © Getty Images
Pages 52-53 Fish eye view of Project Mercury astronaut John Glenn training in a mock up of the planned space capsule, Ralph Morse, 1959. © Ralph Morse/Life Magazine/The LIFE Picture Collection/Getty Images
Page 54 "Great Horned Owl #3, Espanola, NM, 2011," Brad Wilson, 2011. © Brad Wilson
Page 55 "Orangutan #1, Los Angeles, CA 2011," Brad Wilson, 2011. © Brad Wilson
Page 56 Alice Cooper, Michael Ochs, 1970. © Michael Ochs Archives/Getty Images
Page 59 Elizabeth Taylor as Cleopatra in Joseph L. Mankiewicz's film of the same name, 1963. © 20th Century-Fox Film Corp/courtesy Everett Collection
Pages 60-61 Anna Wintour attends the Tom Ford show during London Fashion Week, 2013. © Gareth Cattermole/Getty Images Europe
Page 62 Clark Gable and Vivien Leigh in Victor Fleming's *Gone with the Wind*, 1939. © Everett Collection
Page 63 Frank Sinatra and Vivian Blaine in Joseph L. Mankiewicz's *Guys and Dolls*, 1955. © Everett Collection
Pages 64-65 The crowd is seen during the Yeah Yeah Yeahs performance at the Coachella Valley Music & Arts Festival, Karl Walter, Indio, California, 2009. © Karl Walter/ Getty Images
Pages 66-67 "Open-eyed group," Paul Klee, 1938. © Christie's Images/Bridgeman Images

Pages 68-69 A man hangs off Thomas Jefferson's eye during the carving of Mount Rushmore, South Dakota, c.1930s. © George Rinhart/Corbis via Getty Images
Page 70 James Stewart in Alfred Hitchcock's *Rear Window*, 1954. © Everett Collection
Page 71 Dennis Stock with camera, Andreas Feininger, 1955. © Andreas Feininger/The LIFE Picture Collection/Getty Images.
Page 72 US military personnel wear goggles as they witness a nuclear test, Marshall Islands, 1951. © PhotoQuest/Getty Images
Page 73 Kenneth Willardt, 2015. © Kenneth Willardt/Trunk Archive
Page 74 An image of an eye is projected onto a building by a "skyjector" in New York City, 1960 © F. Roy Kemp/BIPs/Getty Images
Pages 76 - 77 Asia Argento, Milan, Italy, 1996 © Ferdinando Scianna / Magnum Photos
Pages 78 - 79 "Eyes,"Andy Warhol, 1952. © The Andy Warhol Foundation for the Visual Arts, Inc. / Artist Rights Society (ARS), New York
Pages 80-81 Men, women and young children watch a military aircraft flyover on an Armed Forces Day Open House at the Naval Air Station in Lakehurst, New Jersey, 1960. © 1960, Hulton Archive/Getty Images
Pages 82-83 Eyes by artist JR for "Nuit Blanche" art festival, Paris, 2015. © Martine Franck, Paris, France /Magnum Photos
Pages 84-85 Frank Sinatra's *Come Dance With Me* album cover, 1959. © 1959, Michael Ochs Archives/Getty Images
Page 86 Shirley Temple in David Butler's *Bright Eyes*, 1934. © 20th Century-Fox Film Corp/ courtesy Everett Collection
Page 87 Audrey Hepburn in Stanley Donen's *Charade*, 1963. © 1963, Silver Screen Collection/ Getty Images
Page 88 "Evolution of a Bottle in Space," William Wegman, 1999. © 1999 William Wegman
Page 89 "Eyewear" William Wegman, 2001. © William Wegman
Page 91 Jacqueline Kennedy at Barnstable Airport in Hyannis, 1964. © 1964, Bettmann / Getty
Page 92 Model in Gaultier fringe glasses by Richard Burbridge, 2001. © Richard Burbridge
Pages 94-95 Journal Drawing 232, "Les Yeux," Henri Jacobs, 2006. © Henri Jacobs
Pages 96-97 © Jerry Schatzberg / Trunk Archive
Page 99 A fisherman prints an "evil eye" on the prow of his boat to ward off evil spirits in Bombay, Bruno Barbey, India, 1980. © Bruno Barbey/ Magnum Photos
Pages 100-101 Udjat eyes on a coffin, Egypt. © Bridgeman Images
Page 102 Twiggy, Barry Lategan, 1966. © Barry Lategan/Michael Ochs Archives/Getty Images
Page 103 Erwin Blumenfeld, 1938. © 2018 Yvette Blumenfeld Georges Deeton
Page 104 Bette Davis in Edmund Goulding's *Dark Victory*, 1939. © Everett Collection
Page 105 Bette Davis in John Huston's *In This Our Life*, 1942. © Everett Collection
Page 106 Faye Dunaway in Irvin Kirshner's *The Eyes of Laura Mars*, 1978. © Mary Evans Picture Library Ltd./Ronald Grant/Everett Collection
Page 108 Faye Dunaway in Irvin Kirshner's *The Eyes of Laura Mars*, 1978. © Mary Evans Picture Library Ltd./Ronald Grant/Everett Collection

I ONLY HAVE EYES FOR YOU

Published in the United States by powerHouse Books,
a division of powerHouse Cultural Entertainment, Inc.
32 Adams Street, Brooklyn, NY 11201-1021
e-mail: info@powerHouseBooks.com
website: www.powerHouseBooks.com

First edition, 2019

Library of Congress Control Number: 2018962893

ISBN 978-1-57687-819-4

Designed by Krzysztof Poluchowicz

Photo editing by Sarina Finkelstein

Printed by Asia Pacific Offset

10 9 8 7 6 5 4 3 2 1

Printed and bound in China